Your SEAT at the TABLE

Building Trust

A Parable About Public Private Partnerships

Angela Donelson, Ph.D, AICP

with

Jenni Moreno

Published by Entrust Source Publishers

ISBN 978-1-942308-68-3

Cover design by Judy Buckert Entrust Source Publishers

Hand drawn illustrations by Judy Moreno

Entrust Source LLC

Website: www.entrustsource.com

Email: entrustsource@gmail.com

Your Seat at the Table

CONTENTS

PREFACE

The characters and events in this parable are fictional. The patterns they illustrate are not.

These patterns have a name, and so do the experiences behind them: the partner who captured the process while calling it collaboration, the table set for you instead of with you, the moment you realized centralized power was never going to move.

This book names them and lays out an alternative built on the infrastructure that sustains partnerships rather than relying on goodwill that can let them collapse. You'll find a trust-building framework, shared agreements, and accountability structures here that you can adapt to protect your organization, your community and your work.

The book is organized in four parts: the parable, the trust-building theory woven through it, a self-assessment to understand where you can begin implementing steps to build trust in your own partnerships and resources for exploring the concepts further.

Throughout, you'll find simple hand-drawn visuals that illustrate the key principles, designed to be accessible to recreate in your own work.

This is both a story and a field guide.

If you want to go deeper, see our companion workbooks, *The Money Trail: How They Lost It or Stole It* and *Lines You Shouldn't Cross: Privacy, Power and Policy* at entrustsource.com. They equip leaders with field-tested tools and peer-learning case studies grounded in best practices in federal grants management, for self-guided training or alongside coaching.

AUTHORS' NOTE

This book grew out of work we care about deeply: helping organizations build durable, resilient partnerships and holding cross-sector collaborations accountable when personal trust and organizational trust diverge. It is a leadership parable about building and rebuilding those partnerships, grounded in trust and the simple but demanding idea that compliance means doing what you say you will do to mutually agreed standards.

Angela wrote the parable and the trust-building framework woven through it, drawing on a decade of applied research with Dr. Mary Adam at trustforchange.org and her own years in the field. Jenni grounded the compliance measures in the federal Uniform Guidance (2 CFR 200), co-developed the self assessment and visuals and served as contributing editor on the parable. Together we built the companion workbooks.

The parable is a work of fiction. Characters, organizations, locations and events are composites drawn from published accounts, publicly available sources and Angela's professional experience across many years and settings. They do not represent any specific individual, organization or partnership.

We hope this becomes a resource to which readers return, both for thinking through partnerships and as a guide for doing the work.

Disturbed

Maya knew something was off. She couldn't interpret the purpose of the email. The subject line was innocuous: "Desert Corridor Initiative - Next Steps Discussion."

The sender was writing as if someone else had briefed her work, referencing conversations with regional government leadership about "optimization opportunities." How odd and unsettling. Why had they framed it that way?

She pushed back from her desk, irritated. Then she felt a mix of frustration and fear welling up again.

This had to do with the wildlife sensor network. In building it, she had proven that conservation could drive sustainable development and economic returns.

Somewhere in her eagerness to prove the concept, she now felt pangs of remorse. She'd shared a beta version with the partners. Patchy communication followed, then outright silence and now sudden interest from people she'd never met.

She went back to the email. She didn't know the sender, and they weren't writing to her directly. She was just copied, and her original message was buried in the chain.

Someone had asked for her contact information and the project background. Sarah, her partner and trusted sounding board, had provided it. Only she could give Maya context.

She'd been so eager to have this spot at the table. Now, Maya feared she'd somehow given up her seat.

Part 1

The Corridor's Promise

A Way of Life

Maya was the fourth-generation descendant of Western homesteaders and proud of it. Her family had weathered the highs and lows of cattle ranching here even before statehood, filing a land claim everyone else had overlooked. They'd developed a successful operation, picking up a few adjacent parcels here and there when neighbors departed.

In her mid 30s and single, Maya had the time and energy to pour herself into preserving what her family had built. Her two brothers were raising their families and building their businesses on nearby inherited land.

She spent most Sunday dinners with them, watching her nephews grow up amid the wild country she loved. She'd take the boys out to show them the sensors she'd installed, or they'd sit quietly watching for hawks and desert wildlife. They sketched as they watched. She'd just bought the oldest his own notebook.

Maya was an observer first and a builder second. While the rest of her family rushed to fix whatever the storm had broken, she'd spend an hour just watching how the water moved.

Her truck was full of bound leather notebooks. Some were filled with her illustrations of birds and plants, and others with diagrams of sensor placements and migration patterns she was trying to understand. She was fascinated by how technology could reveal what the human eye missed: timing, soil moisture patterns and the invisible threads connecting hardy desert plants and wildlife to scarce water sources.

When she didn't understand something, she'd disappear down internet rabbit holes until she figured it out. She'd always been one to teach herself what she needed to know. Learning and mastering technology was her way of contributing to the family legacy.

It was hard to admit: their way of life was on the decline. So many of their neighbors had sold out. A Canadian intermediary tied to mining interests had begun to buy up properties. They were offering substantial cash payments to those willing to sell. The cash tempted ranchers squeezed by tight margins and it sickened those determined to hold their ground.

They were going to need a plan to keep it in the family. Maya had built one.

Home Again

Maya pushed into high gear as her pickup struggled to reach the ridge of her family's property. She'd thrown her hair into a messy bun that morning, focused on getting out to check the sensors. She wore the same thing as she did most days: jeans, boots, a long-sleeved work shirt and a wide brimmed hat, indispensable in the unforgiving sun.

The valley was awash in color. The panorama was unmatched, seemingly open beyond what the eyes could see.

The rolling hills connecting her family's land to her neighbors were more than desert pasture. Maya saw them as corridors for wildlife.

She had caught the vision in her second year of dual master's studies at the state university. Scraping together funds to attend national conferences and trainings whenever she could, she began to see the potential.

While pursuing an ecology undergraduate degree, she'd spent three summers as a field technician for a desert wildlife research project. She'd hiked remote canyons before sunrise, checked camera traps and troubleshooted monitors. After graduation, they'd offered her a job, and she stayed on two years managing the camera and sensor network.

She'd found their data remarkable: migration patterns no one had documented and wildlife corridors connecting ranch lands. Yet, all that good work seemed to be locked into journal articles and research pilot projects. She'd decided good science wasn't enough. She needed to build something of her own that made conservation profitable for her family. That's what sent her back for the MBA.

Her professors found the combination of business and ecology unusual. Her family called it a phase. Yet, falling commodity prices, industry consolidation and rising land sales over the past several years had changed their minds, especially after she returned with a business plan.

After years of building and testing, she produced proof of concept: the wildlife data revealed migration patterns no one else had documented. They captured rare animals on camera. They were able to develop a pilot tourism program, and those bookings were now solid. Ranchers on nearby properties were interested too, but Maya needed cash to scale.

Learning the Ropes

Getting to this point had been hard. It wasn't hard just for Maya, but the others she'd brought into this work: Ted, Harold and Dusty.

Maya wanted to operate like a business, but she needed a model that treated the land, the ranchers and the community as the bottom line. One of her former professors, Ted Reyes suggested she become a nonprofit. She'd since convinced him and two like-minded colleagues to join the board of her fledgling 501c3.

Maya sat alongside them, all squeezed into the living room of her one-bedroom home. A handful of ranchers were beginning to book experiences and the wildlife data subscriptions were generating revenue. A few others believed in her vision and each gave a couple thousand dollars. Beyond that, they had nothing.

It certainly wasn't enough yet to pay for real office space. Her tiny place doubled as the nonprofit headquarters.

This time, Maya had led them through the financial reports, the expansion timeline and two different scenarios for growth if they could find the money. She was good at this, bridging Ted's big vision with Harold's penny-pinching reality check.

The group was again, unsurprisingly, tired. This board meeting had already run an hour over schedule.

Harold sat with his nylon briefcase at his feet, a few green ledger pads poking out of the top. They'd met a few years ago. He called her after he'd read about Maya's fledgling nonprofit in the local paper.

"You're going to need a bookkeeper before you need a biologist," he'd told her. She knew she needed help and invited him to the next board meeting. He never left.

Today, he was wearing his trademark pressed khaki pants with a short-sleeved button-down in pale blue. His reading glasses hung on a chain around his neck. A retired accountant in his early seventies, he still had the quick energy of someone who'd spent a career catching other people's mistakes.

Harold and Ted were at it again, this time over whether to start saving for an audit.

"We're okay with the books right now, but we're spending more than we should," Harold said, his pen tapping against his notebook. It was a habit he'd developed from decades of working numbers.

"But we need to scale the vision," Ted interrupted.

Ted was lean and graying, in his early fifties, wearing a cardigan over a t-shirt. He pushed his wire-rimmed glasses up his nose as he made his point. "I've watched my former students play it too safe. We've got to spend money to prove this works."

"And I've watched nonprofits implode because they spent too fast," Harold countered. He'd kept the books for half a dozen small nonprofits over the years, including animal rescues, food banks and a community theater. He'd watched three of those fold.

Maya listened, caught between them. Her business degree had taught her financial modeling and market analysis. It didn't prepare her for the wisdom of nonprofit governance, knowing when to heed Harold's caution and when to chase Ted's ambition.

"I need to tell you about an exciting opportunity," Maya interrupted.

Ted and Harold stopped when Maya cut in.

"I've been invited to speak at a conference to people who might have deep pockets," she said.

"Governments and big groups are doing conservation-based economic development. The conference fee's steep, $400. But it's only two hours away, so I can drive there and back the same day."

Dusty looked at Maya and tipped her cowboy hat, her dark eyes steady. She wore a denim work shirt, embroidered with her initials on the collar. A slight woman in her early 60s, she had the steady, capable and no-nonsense presence of someone who'd been running her family's ranch operation for decades.

"That fee is steep. It's half a sensor unit," Dusty said.

Dusty was the board member Maya looked to first. She'd known Maya's family for years and signed up right away when Maya started the sensor tourism program. Ranchers sought her help navigating conflicts with drought and difficult neighbors when tempers ran hot and stakes ran high.

"It may be half a sensor unit, but we can reach a broader audience," countered Ted. "We need more resources."

He gestured with both hands the way he did in his lectures, his sleeves pushed up to his elbows.

"That's proof of concept," he said. "We show impact, the funding follows."

Dusty slowly raised her hand to get Maya's attention.

"Ted's not wrong about the vision," she said, her tone measured. "But vision doesn't keep the lights on when you don't have money in the bank."

Harold folded his arms. "Four hundred dollars is a lot for us right now."

Dusty glanced at him. "It is. And staying invisible has a cost too, Harold. If we don't find real partners soon, we won't have anything left to protect."

Harold paused. "That's true. Maya, I think you should go and learn what's out there. But be careful too. Organizations might want more of what we have than you might want to give."

Harold's words lodged somewhere in the back of her mind, but she was already thinking about the connections she might make and the doors that might open.

She knew Harold saw threats everywhere. She also knew she'd been careful with every decision. It was hard to imagine anyone could take advantage of what they'd built.

Preparing

Maya registered the next day. She threw herself into making a slide deck that probably had too much data and a handout that tried to explain three years of work in five hundred words.

The night before leaving for the conference, she sat in her office reviewing everything again.

Her business plan was sound. The data was strong. The model worked on the ground.

Yet, trying to translate the language of environmental economics into economic development was different. It seemed complicated. She didn't really understand it, so she decided it was probably best not to try. She'd just speak to what she knew.

She packed her laptop and headed out before sunrise the next day, feeling equal parts hopeful and out of her depth.

The Conference Connection

Maya was stuck in gridlock. After a two-hour drive across land the size of Connecticut, she'd forgotten just how bad the traffic could be here at the state capital.

Finally, she broke free from the maze. Pulling up to the conference center, she checked her watch. She had 15 minutes. Approaching the door, she found a mass of people still waiting in line.

Flustered, she raised her hand and waved it. People at the front of the registration table were wearing red badges and sponsorship ribbons.

She caught the eye of one who began walking toward her.

"Can I help you?," the woman asked, approaching with her coffee. "I'm Sarah," she added with a warm smile.

Maya thought Sarah looked a decade older than her. She was warm, approachable and unhurried. Her blazer was professional yet off the rack, hair pulled back efficiently, and she strode confidently forward in simple flats.

"I'm speaking soon. Can you help me find my room?" Maya said.

“What’s your topic?” Sarah motioned them forward as they began walking toward the conference rooms.

“The Desert Corridor Initiative,” Maya stated. “I’m sharing about wildlife monitoring.”

“Wait, you're the one with the wildlife sensor network?” Sarah's interest sharpened. “I've heard colleagues of mine talking about you. I saw your bio in the conference handout.”

“You've actually heard about our research?” Maya's skepticism was evident, as they approached the conference room. “Most people hear 'restoration' and tune out.”

“That’s because they think you're going to lecture them about the environment,” Sarah said. “But you're not doing that. Building something that actually generates money is totally different.”

“I wish I could sit in,” Sarah said, standing at the threshold to the room, “but my agency is a sponsor and I have to head back up to the registration desk to help. Let’s connect after you’re done.”

Coffee

Maya ended her presentation to applause. She felt confident she'd translated her work to an audience that might open new doors.

The regional floodplain and university extension staff were visibly energized by the prospect of jobs and new sources of income.

She had walked them through the key concepts and innovations for their expansion phase. Field technicians would install and maintain weather-resistant sensor stations at strategic points across the corridor. Motion-activated cameras and acoustic sensors would capture wildlife movement and sounds. Water quality monitors would track surface and groundwater, while soil moisture sensors would document ecosystem health. Workers would check, monitor and analyze real-time data. All this could create steady employment for local people.

Her favorite dream innovation, she shared, was cross-training workers to maintain the solar panels powering the remote sensor stations. She hoped it would build a pipeline of higher-paying renewable energy jobs supporting ranching operations.

Tour operators, water conservation managers and federal agencies managing conservation work were also likely buyers, she explained. They needed better real-time monitoring data to track wildlife and the water table.

After answering a few questions and closing her laptop, Maya headed toward the conference registration table. Sarah was waiting, this time with two cups of coffee.

“Let’s head over here,” Sarah signaled to a quiet corner.

“OK, so the subscription model,” Sarah said, cupping her coffee. “How does that actually work? Who's buying in? And where are you finding new clients? Are they finding you?”

Maya answered thoughtfully. She didn’t want to reveal too much yet. She shared her history with the family ranch and the years of proof-of-concept development.

“What I keep coming back to,” Maya said, “is that nobody around here should have to choose between ranching and conservation.”

“So you're from the area,” Sarah said, understanding clicking into place. “This is much more than a project for you.”

“My family’s held land south of here for a long time,” Maya paused. “We're among those who haven't sold, but we need a plan that works.”

Sarah leaned forward. “And it looks like you've built one.”

“On a small scale, yes.” Maya agreed, a bit tentative. “But scaling requires partnerships. That’s why I’m here.”

"Send me your presentation. I've got some meetings this afternoon," Sarah said, checking her phone. "But I'd love to talk more. This is a perfect fit for work we're championing at the Tres Valles Development Authority."

Maya hesitated. "Development authority?"

Sarah's face lit up in a way that told Maya this must be a real passion. "It's my employer. We build economically on what's already here: the land, the people, our really unique environment. We're regional because our challenges are too big for one place, so our connections don't stop at this county's borders."

She paused to scroll through her phone again. "You free next Tuesday, to meet here, my office?"

Maya looked down at her phone. "Sure...10 o'clock?"

"Perfect. Plan for a long lunch!" Sarah smiled.

Tuesday

Maya spent the better part of the week doing research on Sarah and the development authority. She started with their website. Sarah's bio was aligned. She had an undergraduate degree in environmental science and a master's degree in public policy. What interested Maya the most was her skill sets in financing economic development and environmental impact initiatives.

Tres Valles Development Authority seemed focused on advancing those interests. Yet, it was hard for Maya to wrap her head around the organization's structure and operations. Created by a joint powers agreement nearly two decades ago, it had started as a regional planning office and had grown into something harder to define. Three counties operated under the authority of nine elected officials and a professional staff of nearly forty. The electeds convened quarterly and appeared to set priorities. From the dense staff reports and minutes, it seemed that, between meetings, staff ran everything.

Maya studied the org chart further. An executive director reported to the board. Below her sat department directors: economic development, workforce and natural resources. Sarah's name sat under that last department. Her title was Senior Program Manager.

She filed that away and kept reading, delving deeper.

The website had constant references to "public-private partnerships."

That prompted more online research. Maya learned the public sector seemed to need new revenue streams to fund public goods and services. With federal and state governments cutbacks, key services like workforce development and infrastructure were vulnerable. Local government authorities like this one seemed to be left to pick up the tab, driving this hunt for new revenue. Maya found the trend interesting.

Sarah had been doing her homework too. She'd read Maya's slide deck, found a peer-reviewed paper Maya had co-authored and dug into the Desert Corridor Initiative. The more she read, the more she could see their portfolios aligned.

Maya set off for the drive earlier this time. The trip to Tres Valles Regional Development Authority was smooth and traffic-free. The front desk staff let her into Sarah's office. It smelled like coffee and sunscreen. The walls were covered with watershed maps, wildlife photos and groups of smiling youth.

"It's wonderful to have you here, Maya," Sarah smiled warmly.

"Quite a drive, and nice to finally connect!" Maya paused in front of Sarah's desk, looking at the wall.

"Tell me about these pictures?" Maya asked.

"Youth from our workforce programs. We're trying to build a whole workforce interested in and trained for natural resource management. Things are shifting that way," Sarah said proudly.

"That resonates," Maya affirmed.

"I know," Sarah agreed." I've been reading about your work and see you're excited about workforce development too. It's not just your ranch. You're building toward an alternative economy for the whole region."

"We're trying to," Maya corrected. "I'm just someone working with ranchers. We need partners who will invest in the vision."

Sarah's eyes brightened.

"Let's talk the details," Sarah said. "I have lots of questions."

The two sat for hours, poring over slide decks, sharing goals and numbers.

Maya's stomach growled.

"It's 2:30, wow!" Sarah marveled. "Let's get some lunch."

The two headed to the deli down the street.

Building Connection

A week later, Sarah sent Maya an article about failed collaborations in conservation work. The text read: Have you ever seen something like this before?

Maya read it over coffee. It described a multi-year initiative where community partners were promised decision-making power but imploded in broken promises.

She texted back: *Unfortunately yes. A couple of my grad school professors shared cases like this.*

Sarah's response came quickly: *I heard a similar story from Ted Reyes. He's a local professor who supervised one of our intern projects. He published a great case study from work at his prior university.*

Maya sat up straighter. Ted Reyes was on her board. She wasn't aware Sarah knew him.

Maya called her. "Ted's on my board. He's never mentioned working with you."

"He probably wouldn't," Sarah said. "It was years ago, just one summer. But he made an impression. He really went above and beyond. He cared whether our interns actually learned something."

"That sounds like Ted," Maya said.

"He was honest about how hard it is to get partnerships right," Sarah said.

"Those people in his case study failed, not because they didn't care," she continued. "They just didn't see it coming. But that's what happens when people aren't paying attention, when they aren't really engaged."

She laughed a little. "That's not us. We're in on this together, all the way!"

Over the next several weeks and months, they exchanged more. They began to meet. Each conversation seeded new ideas for collaboration. They were aligned.

Reflection

Maya was on the freeway this time, headed north to see Sarah.

Their meetings had long since wandered past business. They traded novels and articles on conservation innovations. Working breakfasts bled into the afternoons.

Sarah talked about Luke, her ten-year-old. She was raising him alone after a messy divorce. Money stress weighed on her, and so did the guilt of never feeling like enough as a mother.

Maya started texting, just small check-ins on her and Luke. Sarah always wrote back.

When they got together, they'd spend an hour on work, then slip into what kept them up at night. Sarah questioned whether the development authority was producing results fast enough. Maya was afraid her projects would collapse under the weight of startup strain and she'd fail the ranchers who trusted her. She was tired of chasing grant funding that rewarded novelty over proven results, and tired of justifying work that was working, just not recognized.

Hands on the wheel, Maya turned over their last conversation, wondering what today would bring.

“I don’t know how much longer I can sustain this pace,” Maya had said, worn out the last time they’d met.

“I know it’s exhausting, trying to chase funds for the work while you’re doing it,” Sarah had affirmed. “But you know what I appreciate about you? You deliver on what you promise. You’re someone I can trust.”

Maya smiled as she remembered, encouraged by what Sarah had shared next.

“I just read this great book by an author named Henry Cloud,” Sarah said. “He’s got a framework for figuring out whether someone is actually trustworthy. Five things to look for.” She paused. “I kept thinking about you the whole time I was reading it.”

“Tell that to the funders I'm chasing,” Maya said.

Sarah laughed. “Seriously. You check every box. Your understanding of this community, your motives, your track record. I've asked around, Maya. The ranchers out here think you walk on water.”

“I'm going to find a way for us to work together. I'm close. I promise.”

Maya held onto that as she drove.

Arrival

Before she knew it, Maya was there.

"You're early!" Sarah said, opening the door warmly to her office.

Maya settled in. Sarah returned from the office kitchen with two well-worn mugs of coffee stamped with the development authority's logo.

She spread out a proposal on her desk. It was a formal partnership agreement with line-item funding highlighted for Maya's nonprofit. The numbers caught her breath.

"It's a multi-year commitment," Sarah explained. "Your innovation, it's at the heart of this."

Maya remained silent, thinking about the implications of not having to think nonstop about funding. This would give her a way to finally just focus on the work.

Sarah continued, "Keep in mind this is our draft pitch to the feds. I've been talking to them. Our ideas are well-matched to their program, and although we think this is amazing, we don't have the money in hand, not quite yet."

"OK," Maya nodded. "Tell me more."

Sarah leaned in. "Tres Valles can provide resources, access to infrastructure, negotiate rights of way. We'd budget for installation of more sensors and equipment, and of course the job training program. You'd maintain control of the technology. We'd like you to collaborate with some nonprofits we've selected, along with property owners, on easements and workforce."

"How many partners?"

"Three others. But I wanted your thoughts first. Without your work, this whole thing is a no-go."

Maya got up to study the pictures on the wall again and the maps. This was going to be bigger than she thought.

"You would set priorities based on needs," Sarah continued. "We'd help you navigate other government agencies and departments, even broker new conversations with federal and state partners. As the sponsor, we'd host meetings, submit proposals and convene the work."

Maya leafed through the proposal. This was real money. The support looked solid.

"This could change the way we work," she said.

"It *will* change the way you work," Sarah affirmed. "I've vouched for you constantly in my upline conversations. We'll create sustainable jobs, generate revenue and restore ecosystems. A triple bottom line."

"You know me, lots of questions," Maya smiled. "This is exciting. I just want to make sure I'm ready for what comes with it."

"Take a look at the proposal," Sarah said.
"If any partner doesn't follow through, we'll build consequences in. Real accountability."

Maya exhaled. This was a lot to take in. Yet Sarah had followed through on small commitments. She knew about Maya's roadblocks and challenges. They'd both shared hard things, personal and professional.

"I'll share with my board," Maya said. "I love it, just need a little time."

"Take a week. We'll be fleshing this out over the next few months. You all need to get to know one another first. More than anything, I'm committed to making this work for you."

Maya relaxed. She felt like she was finally being invited to a table she'd been trying to reach for years.

"Thank you," she said. "Just being considered, that's amazing. I don't have words."

Sarah smiled and then glanced at her watch, her expression turning to mild panic. "Shoot, I've lost track of time. I've got to go get my kid!"

All In

Maya barely remembered the drive home. She sat with the proposal spread across her kitchen table, making notes, already drafting questions for her board.

A couple hours later, she realized it was well past dinnertime. Chopping vegetables for soup, she let herself think. Sarah shared the same values and the same vision. The only real unknown was learning to work with new partners. It was a rare chance to grow, and quickly. She knew she just had to convince her board to take it.

She pulled out her phone and texted Sarah: *Let's schedule a follow-up. I have questions and so will my board, but we'd love to move forward.*

Sarah's response came quickly: *I knew you'd agree. This is going to be so good for the region, Maya. I really believe that.*

Maya looked at the text and nodded. She believed it too.

Part 2

Building

Vetting

Maya knew this meeting was going to be important. She headed out early on the familiar drive north, reminding herself of all she'd done to build the odds for success.

Sarah was up early too. She prepared the development authority conference room for the meeting, wheeling in a portable whiteboard from her office. She pulled a round table out of the supply closet. They rarely used this one, but she needed it. She pushed the rectangular conference table against the wall to make room.

Maya came in first, balancing a thermos of coffee, her laptop and a worn leather notebook. Maya carried this book everywhere. Sarah had seen her filling it up with notes, sketches, maps and organizational charts at meetings, along with doodling in the margins.

"I have to tell you," Maya paused cautiously, as she was first of the group to slide into a chair, "I'm a bit nervous. And it's cold in here," she said as she pulled on her cardigan.

"Yes, they crank up the air. And I'd feel that way too. You're new to this group," Sarah said.

"Thanks," Maya groaned.

"But I think you're going to like them," Sarah acknowledged. "They're good at what they do and care about all this in the same way you do."

A woman in her fifties walked in. She was dressed in a western shirt and well-worn jeans, and her grey hair was pulled back into a ponytail. Her boots were dusty. A silver concha belt caught the light, which Maya later learned was a gift from her grandmother. It had been passed down through three generations of ranching women.

"Sarah! Good to see you," she smiled warmly. She nodded across the room to Maya.

"Carmen, meet Maya," Sarah gestured. "Carmen works with the Preservation Land Trust. She's been helping us with conservation easements with ranchers so we can connect open spaces for wildlife."

Carmen approached. Her handshake was solid. "I've heard amazing things about your work, Maya. My operation's been in the family forty years. Too many neighbors have sold out. We need your thinking, your innovations to make things work."

A moment later Terrence entered, a slight man in his late 20s with a mustache and an easy smile. He wore Adidas and jeans with a Youth Futures polo shirt, sleeves rolled up. He had the restless energy of someone juggling three projects at once.

Sarah introduced him. "Terrence is training young people in construction trades. And moving into green infrastructure, where the jobs are headed."

Terrence grinned, and he set his phone face down on the table. On the back of his phone case was a faded sticker, a youth center logo.

"We've got eighteen kids now," Terrence said. "Most never saw a career path that didn't involve leaving this place! So excited to meet you, Maya.'"

Finally, Marcus arrived, a man in his late 30s. He was stocky and solid, dressed in work pants and a button-down with his company logo, Rural Energy Solutions. His hands were calloused and he carried a loose stack of paperwork on top of his laptop, invoices mixed with site photos.

"Turning these in, Sarah," he said, flustered. "Sorry I didn't have time to grab a folder."

"Marcus is doing solar installations, and with ranchers too," Sarah said, "And we're excited about his energy efficiency retrofits."

Marcus waved from across the table with a smile as he found a seat.

Once everyone was settled, Sarah began.

"We're here to talk about the proposal, due in three months. You've seen the high level draft."

She continued. "Let's first understand what brings us together."

She uncapped her marker. "I've already briefed our other departments on your work. Planning, workforce, conservation. They're impressed. They want this to happen."

She approached the whiteboard and drew a diagram.

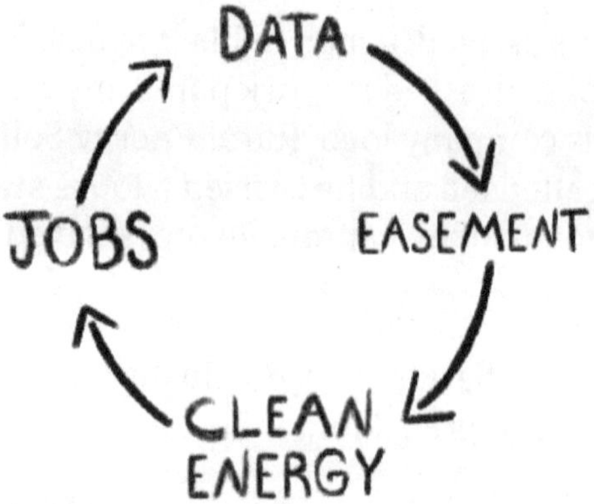

"Maya, you're generating incredible data with ranchers. Carmen, you're preserving habitat with the ranching community through easements. Marcus, you're helping those same ranchers reduce costs through clean energy. And Terrence, you're creating pathways for youth to enter these fields."

She looked around the table. "You're working on different parts of the same system."

Maya opened her leather notebook. "I've been keeping records," she said. "Our sensors pick up more than wildlife. There's soil moisture, temperature shifts, microclimate patterns. I know we weren't framing it that way." She glanced at Carmen. "But it strengthens your case for easements. And Marcus, for solar siting on ranch land."

She closed the notebook. "And it's not just us. Tour operators, water managers, they're already buying subscriptions for wildlife data. We add soil and microclimate monitoring and we're selling something people need. Maybe even to the feds."

The room was quiet for a moment.

Sarah pointed at her. "That. That's why you're in this room."

Marcus sat back. Terrence put his pen down.

Carmen leaned forward. "I want to loop back to what you said about working on parts of a system, Sarah. You're the lead. How do we have a say?"

"Good question," Sarah replied. "The feds want us, a government entity, as lead applicant. That's just how this funding works. I wouldn't have set it up that way, but here we are."

She drew a line at the bottom of the diagram, followed by the word "CONVENER".

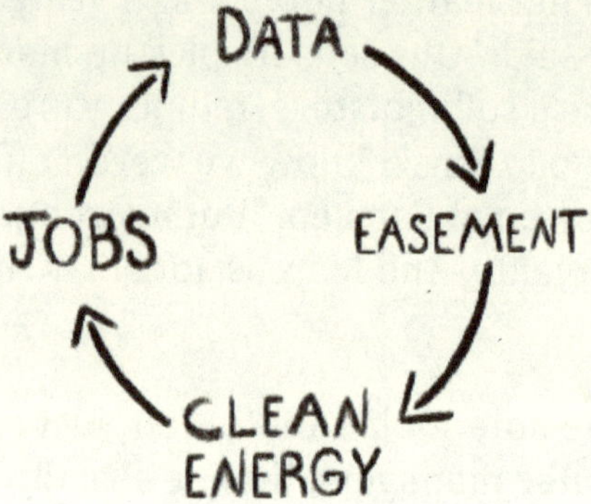

CONVENER

"We need to talk about that word," Carmen said. "It's pretty vague."

"That's fair. So let me be specific." Sarah ticked off on her fingers: "Meeting space. Admin support. Coordinating with other departments. Submitting the federal proposal."

She looked around the table. "That's the development authority's part. The vision and the work? We decide that together."

Maya looked out the window. She still needed more clarity.

Maya ventured. "So, instead of running everything you're more like... the backend support?"

"Yes, backend support, and front end too," Sarah said. "Positioning people, places, resources to support what you do best."

Marcus' frown of concentration disappeared. "You're right. I don't have the bandwidth to pull all that together."

Carmen leaned back and crossed her arms behind her head.

"Sarah, I've been in partnerships before, where the government agency said it was just facilitating," Carmen said.

Sarah met her gaze directly. " I understand where you're coming from."

She reflected before she answered. "I just want to be straight with you. The funder wants us to submit this. Our attorneys have to draft an MOU too. It's important you understand what we have to work with and I want you to trust the process."

"MOU?" Maya asked.

"Memorandum of understanding," Sarah replied. "An agreement among us. We'll get to that more in our next meeting. But for now, I want to talk about Carmen's concern. We're not just facilitating."

She stood up and underlined the word convener.

"Being a good convener means I listen and I advocate for you if you can't be in the room. Your expertise drives decisions." She paused. "And like I said, the other departments and electeds support this."

Maya looked around. Carmen had uncrossed her arms. Marcus's shoulders had dropped a notch.

Maya felt Sarah's words were genuine.

"Sounds great," Terrence said "and I still need to see how this works in action."

"You will," Sarah said. "That's why we've got four meetings ahead to make our federal partner want to fund it. And in between, I'll keep leadership and other departments in the loop."

Carmen raised her hand. "This all sounds fine but how do we know we're all committed to the same high standards? We haven't all worked together."

"That's exactly what we're looking at next," Sarah said, reaching for a stack of papers.

"I've prepared a partner vetting checklist. Take a moment to look it over," she said. She distributed a handout:

VETTING CHECKLIST:

- 501(c)(3) status - in good standing
- Board governance strong
- Federal funds management experience
- Clear mission alignment
- Track record of delivery
- Risk assessment proves readiness and resilience

"This comes straight from the federal funding announcement. It's called a NOFO, Notice of Funding Opportunity. Some agencies say NOFA or RFP. Different names, same thing. It's what the government looks for in those they fund."

She set the handout down. "I've reviewed all your organizations against these criteria. Every single one of you has been working with federal money. That is, except Maya."

"You're right, I haven't," Maya said. "And I need to understand what that lack of experience means...for my nonprofit."

Sarah looked at Maya and paused, continuing, "Definitely, we'll get into that. Don't worry, your work and financials speak for themselves. That's what matters."

"Let's talk about how we meet the requirements," Sarah said. "Let's start with money, since you all need that to make this work."

Each partner shared financial challenges and successes as Sarah took notes. Maya talked about how they had worked on a shoestring budget and managed with a network of mostly volunteers. Carmen shared how the land trust invested in income generating programs. Marcus discussed his experience successfully managing multiple federal grants. Terrence talked about piloting a youth stipend program with the school districts.

"As you can see my organization, the development authority, is not on this list," Sarah said. "We have to vet and manage partners. That's a federal requirement. But we can't do this work without you."

"So we've all managed money and programs," Terrence said. "But none of us have worked together. How do we know that's enough?"

Sarah nodded. "That's exactly what I want to talk about next, why we can trust each other."

Sarah uncapped her marker again. "In the end, it's all really about trustworthiness."

She wrote the word **TRUSTWORTHINESS** on the whiteboard, and underneath it drew five fingers:

"I've been reading and listening to an audiobook by this incredible organizational psychologist, Henry Cloud. He says we need five things for trust. Maya's heard me talk about this already."

She pointed to the thumb on the whiteboard and labeled it.

"Carmen, you've been working with ranchers here for fifteen years. You know their language, culture, their land."

She looked around the room. "When I started making calls about each of you, people didn't just vouch for you. They told me stories. That's understanding."

Carmen laughed, "They probably told you too many stories...for me at least."

Terrence tilted his head and grinned. "That kind of looks like a turkey."

Sarah smiled. "You're right. That'll make it easier to remember!"

The index finger came next. She titled this one GOOD MOTIVES.

"This one's about your intentions," Sarah said. "What are you after? Marcus, when I called your past clients, they all said the same thing. You could have pushed them toward the most expensive solar energy systems, but you always recommended what actually fit their needs and budgets.

She set the marker down. "Nobody in this room is here to get rich. You're here because you care."

Marcus crossed his arms. "I mean, I wouldn't mind getting paid fairly for the work. But yeah, that's not why I'm here."

She tapped the middle finger next. She titled it, ABILITY.

"Can you deliver what you promise? Terrence, I pulled your program data before I ever picked up the phone. Ninety percent job placement rate."

“Carmen, your easement portfolio has protected more acreage than some state programs. Maya, I had two federal reviewers look at your sensor methodology. They couldn't poke a hole in it.”

Terrence shifted in his chair. “Where'd you get ninety? It's ninety-three.”

Sarah pointed the marker at him. “Even better.”

Sarah paused and added a fourth label, CHARACTER, over the ring finger.

“Are you honest and upfront about your limitations?

Maya, you've been clear from day one about what you can and can't do. You underplay your hand yet ranchers I've talked to think you walk on water. You're all leaders of character."

She looked at the group. "I've done my homework on all of you. Not one person said you'd overpromised. Not one."

Maya pushed her chair back slightly from the table. "I'd rather lose a deal than lose someone's trust."

Carmen nodded. "Once it's gone, you don't get it back. Not out here."

Finally, she turned to the whiteboard to label the pinky: TRACK RECORD.

"Do you produce results? Every single one of you has years of outcomes. You've all delivered. In spades."

Sarah set down the marker. "We need a lot of trust to do this work together. And you all need to know how rare this is."

They talked next about how each would handle anticipated challenges. That was important to their last item on the vetting checklist, the risk assessment.

Sarah paused before they continued. "Here's what you need to understand about federal funders and risk. They want proven models that work but need scaling up. They don't want to fund experiments that might break, they want track records with backup plans that show you've thought through what could go wrong."

She gestured at the circle. "That's why this conversation matters. We need to show them you've all done this before, just not together at this scale."

They brought up potential points of failure and how they would handle them in the proposal.

Sarah took notes as Carmen described a failed easement negotiation and what she'd learned. Now she involved whole families in early negotiations and gave them six months to decide. Marcus talked about a solar project that failed when partners didn't communicate. He responded by building weekly check-ins into every contract. Maya shared her early struggles with rancher trust and how she'd now learned to listen for months before proposing anything. Terrence described losing youth participants who couldn't get to job sites. He now partnered with a transit partner and built a volunteer driver network as backup.

At lunch, they were still energized. They planned their next meeting and exchanged cell numbers in a group chat.

"This felt good," Marcus reflected as they packed up. "I've been in lots of these kinds of meetings. This one felt different."

"That's the point," Sarah said. "That's why I brought up trust. If we can't talk about that first, we won't survive the big stuff later."

"One last thing before we wrap up," Sarah urged, pulling two sets of colored index cards out of a rubber band, "Let's do a simple homework assignment for our next meeting."

Terrence raised an eyebrow. "Homework already?"

"We have lots to do," Sarah said as she handed each of them two cards. "Let's come back to our next meeting in two weeks, ready to answer two questions."

"OK?" Carmen prompted.

"First," Sarah paused, "what do you do better than anyone else? Second: What do you need from this partnership you can't do alone?"

Maya turned the cards over. They were blank, waiting.

"That's it?" Marcus asked.

"That's it. You'll identify one strength, one need. Write it down and bring it back." Sarah began gathering her things. She glanced at her watch.

"I've got after-school pickup, I'm almost late already. So let me wrap this up," she paused, smiling. "When I write this up, I already know we'll have a home run."

Maya looked through the window at the mountains in the distance. She thought about her sensor networks, the years of relationships with ranchers and the technical expertise she'd built. She thought about the gaps and how she needed to grow her partnerships into something bigger.

Terrence tucked the card into his notebook. "I can work with this." he said. "And two notecards, that's not enough."

"Okay," Sarah said. "Let's meet back here, two weeks. Same time, same place. And next time I'll bring churros from that new place near my house."

Sarah hurried out. The others lingered.

Maya slipped the cards into her bag.

She knew what she'd write on the first card. The second one was harder. She had answers, but this was a new table. She wanted to see how everyone else played their cards first.

Coffee with Carmen

Maya woke up knowing what was next: she needed to see partners operating in their element.

She texted Carmen. *Can I come out to your ranch this week?*

Carmen's reply came fast: *Thursday. Wear something you don't mind getting dirty.*

Two days later, Maya found herself bouncing down a dirt road in Carmen's old truck. The shocks were well worn, as it had seen better days and certainly better decades.

"You want to understand what we bring to this?" Carmen asked, one hand on the wheel, and another on the stick shift. "We have a success story. The ranchers out here finally know conservation easements help them. Finally...that we aren't stealing their land."

They pulled up to a gate. Carmen jumped out, unlocked the hitch and kicked it open with her well worn boot in one fell swoop. It looked like something she had done at least a thousand times.

"Do you know the hardest part?" Carmen asked as she got back in the truck.

"What's that?" Maya asked.

"It's not legal paperwork. Not the appraisals. It's sitting at someone's kitchen table and getting them to trust you. Listening as they share their fears. They're all worried about keeping their land in the family."

Maya took notes in her leather notebook.

"That's just like ranchers I work with too," Maya said.

"I've learned," Carmen said as she put the truck back into gear, "I can talk about wildlife corridors in ways that make sense to them. I don't pretend to know all the answers. They know I'm learning with them."

Maya agreed. "It's taken time for them to trust me too."

"You know what this is like," Carmen said. "I'm glad you'll get to visit a couple of them today."

They hit a washout that sent Maya's notebook sliding off the dash. Carmen caught it without looking and handed it back.

"Sorry about the road. County keeps saying they'll grade it. Not likely."

Maya felt grounded even as the truck continued to bounce hard.

More Site Visits

Marcus and Terrence were next, and like Carmen, both were eager to show what they'd built.

Marcus walked her through a solar install. The rancher persisted with the same question about his meter reading. Marcus answered it three times without changing his tone. On the drive back he said, "I've turned down jobs where the client didn't need what they were asking for. They shouldn't be paying for what they don't need. Word gets around."

Terrence led her on a tour of his youth center. Halfway through, they met up with one of his high schoolers running wire through conduit. He had pulled it too hard, jamming it halfway. Terrence didn't touch it.

"What's your next move?" He prompted.

The kid relaxed, backed the wire out and fed it through again, slower, until it cleared.

Afterward, Terrence told Maya that a foreman in South Philly had given him the same chance when he was sixteen.

"The only job I could get was demolition," Terrence said. "He saw something else in me and moved me to electrical. I'm here because of that guy."

Maya walked away grateful, aware that like Marcus and Terrence, she didn't try to fix everything. They understood their role as being present, helping others figure things out themselves.

Her thoughts turned to Sarah, who had been following their work for some time. Sarah asked about specific camera placements, seemed to understand why certain migration corridors mattered and easily connected the wildlife data to the bigger conservation picture. Most people nodded politely when Maya talked about her work. Sarah tracked it with real interest.

And then at their last meeting, Sarah had remembered it was Maya's birthday. Maya had mentioned it once, weeks back. Not many people remembered anymore. Her brothers were busy with their own families and her friends from college had scattered. Sarah had brought a potted native plant for her porch. "I saw this and thought of you," she said. It felt like the kind of thing a real friend would do.

When she sat down that evening to finish Sarah's homework assignment, the ideas came easily. They flowed beyond the two index cards into her leather bound notebook.

Agreements

Everyone was early this time. Sarah had her whiteboard ready. She'd put a draft Memorandum of Understanding at their places alongside a basket of churros.

"The attorneys just got this to me last night," Sarah said, looking at them apologetically after everyone arrived. "I meant to get it to you before the meeting. So sorry. Let's take 10 minutes to read it through and then we can dig in. That okay?"

They all nodded in agreement.

Maya thumbed through her copy, as did the others, in silence. It wasn't too long, she thought, only 12 pages. The language seemed straightforward. She'd have her board look it over too.

Carmen was already flipping to the back. "Can we just get to who does what?" she said.

"Sure. That's page 3." Sarah got her marker out.

She divided the whiteboard into columns, a name at the top of each. They spent an hour going over the details: who owned what, and what each needed to make it work.

Maya took technology and training coordination; she needed funding and federal experience she didn't have. Carmen owned landowner relationships and conservation planning; she needed partners who could make the broader case. Marcus carried energy audits and installation; he needed career pathways for his graduates. Terrence held the youth pipeline through job placement; he needed data to prove it was working. Sarah wrote her own name in the last column: grant administration, government liaison, convener.

She set the marker down. On a fresh corner of the whiteboard, she drew the convener diagram again, the same one from their last meeting. "Now look at how these roles connect."

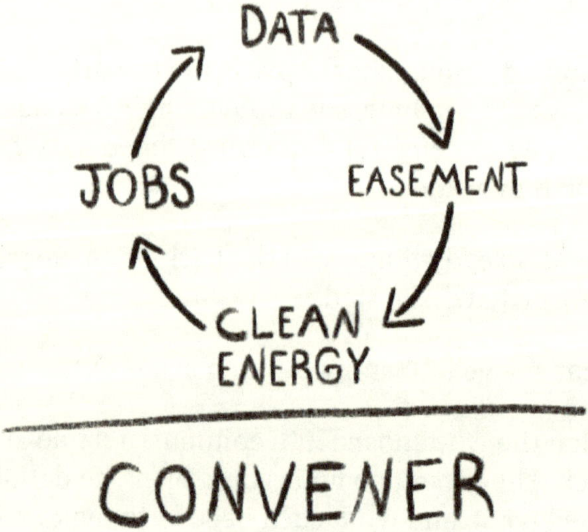

Maya looked at it, then back at the columns. "So when we make decisions, how do we bring equal weight?"

"Good question. Page five," Sarah said. "The development authority has one vote, like everyone."

"One vote," Terrence smiled. "I could get used to that."

Two hours into the meeting, Sarah walked around the room with the coffee pot, refilling their empty cups.

"Still with me?" she asked. "Because this next part has teeth."

She asked them to flip to page eight. "If any partner fails to meet milestones, the others can vote to remove them from the partnership."

"So that happens if one of us can't or won't deliver?" Terrence asked.

"Yes, any one of us," Sarah said. "Even us, the development authority."

"That's strong," Terrence said.

"It's a real commitment," Sarah said. "And how it works, the MOU gets us to the contract. Once we have funding, everything we're agreeing to here is in place."

"So it's not a contract, not binding yet?" Terrence asked.

"Not quite. Our legal requires this first when we work with partners on federal funds," Sarah said. "Since we're the responsible party, we use this process. It's standard for this funding."

That seemed to make sense, Maya thought. The MOU first, which they all would sign, followed by a contract after they won the funding.

"And intellectual property?" Marcus probed.

Sarah flipped to the following page.

"That's next. Page 9: Communications and Proprietary Information," she read, pausing until everyone was there. "The collaborative will protect proprietary information received in the course of implementation." She looked up. "Standard language, but important."

"I know my board. I'll need to get their input," Marcus said.

The others murmured agreement.

"Of course," Sarah said. "Loop them in this week. We've got a little runway still."

Next were the dispute resolution procedures and exit clauses. Scanning around the table, Sarah could see everyone was worn down.

"These are pretty standard legal things," Sarah said. "If you have questions, get them to me by next week. The attorneys need a few days to respond so we can sign next time."

Just as they were winding down, Sarah's phone buzzed, a different ringtone.

"It's the school," Sarah said. "Hold on just a minute. I need to step out and answer it before we wrap up."

A few minutes later, Sarah returned. Her face was strained and her right hand trembled as she held her phone.

"There's been an accident," she said, clearly shocked. "'I've got to go. It's Luke."

She looked at them for a moment, then was out the door.

News

The others walked to their cars in awkward silence. Maya sat with her hands on the wheel, then took out her phone and texted Sarah.

"Sarah, I am so sorry. I'm here if you need anything."

She drove home.

Hours later, Sarah hadn't responded. Maya camped out in front of her TV and eventually dozed off.

The next morning, a text was waiting.

"Maya, Luke is at Mission Canyon Hospital. He fell off the monkeybars and broke his tibia. Scheduled for surgery this morning. I'd love some company if you have time. This is scary."

Maya winced. She thought about her nephews, how worried her brothers would be if something like this happened to them.

She texted back: *I am so sorry on my way. I'll bring you lunch.*

The Hospital

A nurse led Maya down the hallway. She noticed the faint smell of bleach while the fluorescent lights hummed above.

"Watch your step," the nurse waved as she pointed toward the cones set up by the cleaning crew.

Maya approached the room. Peeking in, she could see Sarah was holding Luke's hand. He was sleeping.

Maya entered and set down the paper bag she was carrying with Sarah's thai curry, her favorite.

"Thanks so much," Sarah sighed wearily. "I was hungry."

"You've been through it," Maya said, as she gave Sarah a quick hug. "How is he?"

"The surgery went well," Sarah stated, explaining that a specialist had seen him that morning. "He'll need a lot of physical therapy because of where that break is, but he's going to be okay."

They spoke for a while about work.

"I have a new boss," Sarah said quietly. "Jeff. He came from the private sector just three weeks ago. Already everything's metrics and timelines."

"That sounds hard," Maya said.

"And now this." Sarah gestured at Luke. "I need time off right when I can't be distracted."

She set the carton of food aside and sank back against her chair. "Thanks for being here."

It *did* feel good to be here, Maya thought. She hadn't been asked to fix anything, but just show up.

Luke stirred and opened his eyes. He looked small in the hospital bed.

"Hey, buddy," Sarah said softly. "You haven't met my friend Maya. I've told you about her, remember? She tracks cool animals!"

Luke nodded groggily.

Maya pulled her chair slightly closer to the bed. "Would you like to see one?" she said, ready with her phone.

She swiped through several photos. First was a family of javelinas at dawn and then some roadrunners. She stopped at the one that made Luke's eyes widen.

"Is that a cat?" he asked.

"It's a video of a bobcat," Maya said.

Luke studied the footage, the spotted cat moving through the wash and cottonwood trees.

"That's so cool," he said with a wide smile.

Maya showed him pictures of how the cameras worked and answered questions about what the animals did at night.

Sarah watched, her shoulders relaxing.

After a while, Luke's eyes grew heavy again. He drifted back to sleep.

"Thank you," Sarah whispered. "He's been pretty scared."

"I'm glad I could help. I'm on call for errands, groceries, whatever you need," Maya said. "Anytime."

She thought about her nephews, how she loved entertaining them, and how Sarah was doing all this on her own.

"I appreciate that," Sarah replied. "I'll be taking sick leave to be with Luke, so we'll be okay. It's just the timing of this couldn't have been worse."

A Green Light

As she got ready to leave the hospital, Maya sent a quick group text to her board.

We have an MOU with the development authority. They need a response within the next day or two. I'll email it to you. Can you talk soon?

After some back-and-forth, they scheduled a four-way phone call.

As they began, Dusty was enthusiastic "This project gives us runway we've never had."

They went over the details. Ted was supportive. It was Harold who gave her pause.

"This is a pretty good agreement," Harold said. "But it's thin on some of the details. Not enough time for an attorney review. Maya, how do you feel? Do you think you can trust them?"

"I do," she said. "We've spent months together and others have worked with Sarah before. I've done site visits. Partners are doing good work."

Dusty pointed out the obvious. "Good. We really just don't have more time here."

"I think we have to go with it," Ted said. "The contract follows."

Dusty weighed in. "Not much else to do then. You've really brought us something amazing, Maya."

Maya exhaled. She hadn't realized she'd been holding her breath.

Check In

The next morning, over her first cup of coffee, Maya sent Sarah a text.

How's it going? Need any help?

Several days later, Maya heard back.

Would love to check in. Luke's home with a sitter while I take care of some things. Can you meet in half an hour at the diner?

Maya arrived with some chapter books she'd bought and a book about big cats of the Americas, along with some snacks.

"Luke will love these," Sarah smiled.

They talked about Sarah's workload and Luke's therapy. She'd been granted a remote work pass until Luke was back in school full time. Her new boss was still hard to read, she said, but supportive.

Sarah seemed to want to say something else but didn't. As Maya looked at her, she noticed the dark circles under her eyes, sharp in the light through the window.

"You look exhausted," Maya said softly.

Sarah tensed, "And I've got a ton of medical appointments for Luke and some big bills to pay…" she trailed off.

Maya asked, "How can I help?"

Sarah was quiet for a moment. Then she straightened and changed the subject.

She wanted to know more about the sensor technology for the federal application: the deployment details, data specs, more than she'd ever asked.

"I still have to make progress on this," she said. "We're still meeting next week."

"Are you sure?" Maya countered. "I'm happy to do some writing for you, help you out."

"No I've got it," Sarah stated, gazing out the window. "I have to, that's what my boss made crystal clear."

The conversation turned to data collection protocols and equipment maintenance. Sarah was taking notes. She took screenshots of the front and back-end systems.

"Can you send me a beta version to study for the proposal?" she asked.

"I'll email it tonight," Maya said.

Then Sarah gathered her things, thanked her, and was gone.

Signing the MOU

A week passed. Maya entered the room, ready to sign the MOU. Terrence, Carmen and Marcus were waiting. Sarah was late.

Carmen opened. "We're willing to move forward. We wanted more time, but okay waiting for the contract."

Terrence, Marcus and Maya shared their respective boards had decided to do the same.

Sarah arrived, first with good news. Luke was recovering.

"That's such a relief," Marcus said. The others murmured agreement.

Sarah smiled, then got to business: the development authority would be submitting their application in three weeks. She passed around a copy of the MOU signature page. They discussed and signed. The electronic copy would follow by email later in the week, she said. It was not quite ready yet.

As they were about to close, Sarah looked up and into the hallway.

They could hear two men deep in conversation.

Maya caught fragments of their exchange, something about 'power' and 'infrastructure' and 'utility' partnerships." One mentioned 'data capacity.'

Their voices had that practiced confidence, dropping buzzwords like they were closing a deal. The voices grew quieter as they approached the doorway.

Sarah smiled as they peeked in, one Maya thought looked slightly forced.

"Everyone, this is Cliff Austin Davis, County Supervisor and Development Authority chair, and our new director, Jeff Brooks," she said.

"Cliff and Jeff, this is our dream team," Sarah said, waving her hand toward the group. "Our Desert Corridor Initiative."

Jeff smiled briefly and held back in the corner, offering a quick wave.

Cliff made his way around the room with enthusiastic handshakes. "So nice to meet you," he said.

Maya couldn't help but notice his gold cufflinks which caught the light with monogrammed initials: CAD.

"You're doing exciting work!" Cliff beamed. "Sarah's been keeping me updated. We'll make this succeed."

He checked his watch, also gold plated. "I have to run to another meeting. So good to put a face to our support. Y'all keep up the good work."

After the two departed, Marcus was the first to speak. "That's your boss?"

"That's my boss' boss," Sarah clarified. "My boss was in the corner."

"Those cufflinks," Carmen murmured.

She shook her head. "Now that's branding."

Sarah smiled despite herself.

"Cliff's a politician," Sarah said, her face relaxing a bit.

"If you can believe it, he even has a matching gold pen, a gift from the governor, with his initials."

She glanced at her watch and headed out the door, "I'm sorry, I've got to go, Luke's got an appointment. You'll hear from me over email. We'll go over the final draft together."

Cooling Off

The next morning, Maya texted Sarah.

How are you? How about my house for a change of scenery?

Sarah suggested they meet at the coffee shop near Tres Valles Regional Development Authority office instead of Maya's place.

Easier, her text said. *Crazy week.*

Maya ordered them both coffee and was waiting in the back corner. Sarah arrived checking her phone. She slid into the chair still looking at the screen.

"I've had back-to-back meetings all morning," she glanced up briefly. That tense body language was back.

Maya wasn't sure what to say, so she let Sarah lead.

Sarah wanted to review the sensor data again for the proposal. This time her questions went deeper. She asked how often the sensors transmitted and about data storage capacity. She also asked whether she could test remote access to the cameras.

Maya paused. "Remote access? You need that?"

"Just for the technical section," Sarah said, briefly looking up from her phone. "I have some questions about how it works."

Maya waited for more. Nothing came.

"I was thinking we could plan a field visit for the whole group. Get everyone out to the sites together before the proposal goes in?" she ventured.

"Great idea," Sarah said, still scrolling. "We'll talk about it next time."

Sarah's phone buzzed. She glanced at it, looked at Maya and sighed.

"I'm so sorry, got to run for a meeting with my boss," she said, already heading for the door, leaving her coffee mostly untouched on the table.

Maya stayed, her own coffee cooling. Sarah had said she had a remote work pass to take care of Luke. So why was she in the office again, running back-to-back meetings all morning?

She couldn't name it yet, but she felt it, like a door closing before the lock clicks.

Waiting

Two weeks from the deadline, there was still no proposal.

Carmen texted the group: *What's going on?*

Maya had heard nothing either.

She texted Sarah again: *Let's catch up. I know you've been working hard. I'll get you a sitter.*

The next day Sarah replied: *Maya, so sorry, can't do it. Let's take a rain check.*

Maya responded: *That's alright, let's plan another time. How's next week?*

Next week came. She still heard nothing.

When Maya finally got her on the phone, Sarah's voice was distant and distracted.

"I know. I've been terrible. There's just some internal things going on," Sarah said. "It will all be fine and we'll get this in."

"Will we make the deadline?" Maya asked pointedly.

“Definitely, I know we’re running a little late but I’ll get you all something tomorrow. Not due ‘till next week and we’ve got a great draft,” Sarah said.

“We’ll get there. Gotta run!”

Letdown

That was yesterday. Now, Maya sat in her home office as light faded over the hills. She opened her laptop. Could she make sense of this?

She pulled up the email threads with Sarah. They explained the growing unease she'd felt the past three weeks.

"Can't make our meeting - swamped."

"Love the sensor data. Am using it for our proposal. Let's reconnect soon."

"Still working on those details. Hang tight!"

Sarah hadn't answered some of Maya's messages at all.

Breadcrumbing.

That's what Dusty called it when Maya finally called her.

Maya needed someone who could read people, who'd navigated enough deals and agreements to know when something was off. Dusty had dealt with plenty of folks who talked big and delivered small.

"Tell me what's happening," Dusty said.

Maya laid it all out over the phone.

"It's just like dating," Dusty said. "They keep you hoping, working, filling in the gaps. And then they just stall."

She'd seen it in ranching too, she said. The powerful ones always played it the same way.

"It's not you," she affirmed. "It's them, something's changed. We need to get the board together to talk."

Maya looked it up.

Breadcrumbing: offering someone just enough attention to maintain their interest, getting just what they need to keep you on the hook.

It was a trail leading nowhere.

Maya reflected. Eight months ago, Sarah had come to her with high hopes and promises of a multi-year commitment. Maya had refocused everything around it.

They'd gotten to know each other outside of work too. Now Maya tried to remember: had Sarah actually shared as much as she'd thought? Or had she read reciprocity into nods and acknowledgments?

Maya felt the sinking feeling deepen. Her data, her relationships, her innovations, all an open book. She'd trusted Sarah with friendship. That was what Sarah had labeled it. Was that really true?

She now sat with anger and frustration heavy in her stomach. Then, it turned to embarrassment. How quickly she'd been to trust.

Who to Call?

Now that Dusty knew, Maya wondered who to contact next. The rest of the board or her partners?

She settled on her board first.

She fired off a text to Harold, Ted and Dusty: *"We need to meet. Something's not right with the development authority."*

Her mind circled. Somewhere in their government offices, this proposal and this work were buried, but why?

Her phone buzzed.

It was Harold: *Dusty's filled us in a bit. When and where? I'll bring food.*

Ted: *Your house, Maya. I've got a lot to share.*

Dusty: *Tomorrow night.*

She confirmed with a mix of worry and relief. The realization set in: this was not just about her. This was about her board, the ranching relationships and the community. It was going to be hard, but at least she wasn't alone.

The Email

Maya woke up early the next morning, thinking about her meeting today and what she'd need to do to prepare.

Then, she remembered something. Not yet out of bed, she flipped open her laptop.

She opened the email. It had come after Luke's accident, shortly after she'd shared her beta version of the data with Sarah.

It read: *Desert Corridor Initiative - Next Steps Discussion*.

Given the events of the past two weeks, Maya now understood it differently. It came from a sender she didn't know referencing "optimization opportunities."

She'd been copied by accident.

She scrolled to the bottom of the chain. Someone had asked Sarah for Maya's contact information and background on the sensor network. Sarah had forwarded it all, but no one ever reached out.

She closed her laptop.

She'd been so eager to have a seat at their table. Now the ghosting made sense, if that's what this was. The embarrassment and shame returned.

Could she fix this?

Part 3

The Revelation

Emergency Session

Everyone arrived at 7 p.m. sharp. Harold brought tamales from the place near the highway, knowing this would probably be a marathon session.

Ted came in balancing a towering stack of documents propped up under his chin.

Dusty followed with a couple bottles of Chardonnay in one hand and a giant thermos of coffee in the other.

"Figured we'd need both. Ted says we have a long night ahead," she said, entering the door.

"What are these?" Maya asked Ted as he placed the stack of papers on her living room table. It had been a long time since she'd seen, much less worked with, a pile of papers that high.

"It's fruit of a public information request," Ted replied. "We're dealing with the public sector here, so it's all paper rather than a digital file. Seems like they're stuck with computer systems from the 90s."

"But why bring all this in the first place?" Maya asked.

Ted went on to explain how a coalition of his former students had been filing public information requests for months. They'd started hearing tips connected to a flurry of activity with the Tres Valles Development Authority: unusual land acquisitions near the county's main electrical substation, water rights quietly shifting to industrial use and a joint press release with the utility company promising a forthcoming 'transformative infrastructure investment.'

"Alone maybe those things aren't a big deal," Ted said, "But when you start connecting the dots, we've found it seemed to point to something bigger. One of my students reached out to a reporter who'd been covering rural development deals across the West."

Ted pulled out his phone and showed Maya a screenshot of an email thread. "The reporter's following the money here and other places too, tracking LLC formations, corporate board connections, and how certain players keep showing up in these deals. His work plus ours fit together like puzzle pieces."

Ted went on to explain that Jeff and Cliff, whom Maya had met at their last meeting at the development authority, appeared to be at the center of a major economic development deal. Maya remembered them both, especially Cliff, the elected official with the gold cufflinks.

The room was beginning to take its own momentum now. Maya could feel her window closing.

"I'd actually been the one to call this meeting..." she said. "I want to bring up what I'd called us for."

She felt the pangs of remorse and shame return, feelings that overwhelmed her earlier that morning. She wasn't ready. She took a deep breath and continued.

"..But this is explosive...you're right, Ted," she conceded. "We need to hear it. So keep going."

Ted gestured to the stack. "So when we suspected something was happening, my students filed these public records requests, producing this right here."

They gazed at the pile, leaning slightly under its own weight.

It was bristling with neon post-its. Ted provided context: pink ones flagged conflicts of interest, yellow ones highlighted contractual problems, and green ones signaled what he called 'smoking guns.'

Harold reached over and picked up the top few pages. "There's always a money trail," he said, almost to himself.

Dusty eyed the green post-its. "That's a lot of green for an economic development deal."

She set down the thermos. "Seems like a long night. Let's eat first."

Follow the Money

They piled their plates high as Maya brought out chips and salsa to share.

"Get comfortable," Ted said, leading the group from the kitchen into the living room. "This is going to be quite a ride."

They settled into the sofas and chairs.

Ted divided the stack into two piles. He took a couple post-its out of the middle sections.

"I'm going to walk you through how foreign companies use public-private partnerships to extract value from our community. All in the name of job creation," Ted said.

He went on, hand on the first pile.

"This first stack shows Tres Valles working hand in glove with the power company," Ted said. "They're conversations that justify rate increases for all of us."

"A hyperscale data farm deal," he said. "They're pitching it as tech and jobs. But these two piles together tell one story."

"Data farms?" Maya asked.

"Warehouse-sized facilities packed with servers. They need land, lots of it, and constant massive power." Ted paused. "Our power company loves customers like these. Expands their base, literally."

Dusty stood up. The room got quiet.

"I've been following operations like these elsewhere," she said. "They compete with us as ranchers for water and electricity and drive up demand, and then we're the ones who can't afford what's left."

Maya looked at Dusty, then Ted.

"Then why is the development authority pushing this?" Maya asked. "They're supposed to be working for us."

"Because," Ted paused, "there's just too much money involved."

Harold leaned back. "Like I said, always a money trail," he said quietly.

Trojan Horse

Ted circled the table and picked up a paper-clipped section from the second stack, tabbed with all three colors of post-its.

"This," he warned, "is language for a power-data farm contract that, if approved, screws the community. It promises $500 million in tax revenue over twenty years."

Harold looked up from his legal pad. "Revenue...based on what model?"

"That's the thing," Ted said. "Black box economic impact modeling. Consultants plugged numbers into a formula, and no one could see the assumptions or check the math."

"So the development authority bought into a half-billion dollar projection they didn't fully vet," Harold said.

"Right. And the underlying theory," Ted said, "is that when a company sets up shop, workers spend locally, suppliers do business here, the benefits ripple out. That's not how these data centers work. What stays here is a fraction of what gets extracted."

"And if you can believe it, some internal memos show development authority staff actually tried to get their partners to float industrial revenue bonds to attract this deal."

Ted was met with blank looks.

"Think of it as our government co-signing a loan for a private company," he explained. "The company gets cheap financing. Taxpayers are on the hook if things go south, for decades."

Harold shook his head. "Early in my career, I worked with a firm that audited governments carrying decade-old bond debt for facilities that closed years ago," he said. "It's ugly."

Ted thumbed forward to a page buried with yellow post its.

"The draft language for the legal agreement," he said, "is so lopsided it's truly stunning."

He put on his reading glasses and read:

The Developer may, at its sole discretion, waive any and all performance conditions enumerated in Section 4, subsections A through G, without penalty or renegotiation of lease terms.

He paused, letting the words settle.

Tres Valles Regional Development Authority agrees that such waiver shall not constitute grounds for delay, modification, or termination of this agreement.

"It's all a one-way escape hatch," Ted explained. "The developer can waive studies for impacts we can't even anticipate."

He set the papers down.

“Hyperscale data farms like this one generate massive heat. Some communities now see temperature spikes in certain neighborhoods, microclimates shifting. Researchers are starting to document this stuff.”

Dusty shook her head.

“And here's one nobody saw coming,” Ted continued. “A town in Texas, about our size, landed one of these megaprojects. They were sold on the construction jobs, local spending, the usual pitch. What actually happened? Thousands of workers showed up from out of town. Rents shot up overnight. Even some families ended up on the street.”

“I read something similar last month,” Harold said. “Once it's built, a few technicians run the whole thing. The workers leave. The rents don't come back down.”

He set his pen on the pad. “The company gets the asset. The community absorbs every cost.”

Dusty had been quiet through most of it. “What about water?” she asked.

“Their cooling systems recycle water over and over,” Ted said. “The treatment chemicals get more concentrated every cycle. At some point they risk contaminating groundwater. Health and noise impacts, those are concerns too just now starting to be documented.”

Dusty looked at the table. She knew all too well what contaminated groundwater did to rangeland.

He flipped to a green tab near the back, one of the 'smoking guns.'

"Here's the real kicker. Section 12.3." He read slowly:

Upon provision of ninety days written notice, Developer retains the unilateral right to terminate this agreement at any time following the third year of operation, without penalty, liability or obligation to remediate or restore the subject property to its prior condition.

Maya set down her plate of tamales. "They can just leave?"

"After three years, yes. And when this data center craze crashes, the development authority will probably be left with a hulking structure they can't demolish or afford to maintain."

Ted pulled out his phone and showed her an article he'd bookmarked.

"The industry is already pivoting to nuclear-powered facilities. No place in this country can handle these energy loads."

Ted shuffled the stack back into a pile.

"And somehow, we're all supposed to call it economic development," he said.

"How does any of this stuff get approved?" Maya asked.

"It's a Trojan horse," Ted said. "They dress it up as a gift to the community. A community benefits agreement. And listen to this."

He fished through the stack for a page tagged in all three colors and read:

Digital Harvest Solutions agrees to disburse $10 million annually to the community for three years, with community input, at Digital Harvest Solutions' sole discretion.

Maya crossed her arms. "$10 million dollars a year?"

"For three years," Ted said, "And revocable with thirty days' notice. They control everything."

"That feels like hush money," Harold said. "Drop in the bucket. Buying social license to operate."

Dusty set down her glass. "Social license is right. This isn't legal permission. It's whether the community will tolerate you. In ranching, if neighbors think you're overgrazing or fouling water, you're out."

"So they're buying acceptance with pennies on the dollar," Maya said.

"And they'll sprinkle some good deeds around the community," Dusty added. "Fund a Little League team here, some big school events, a senior center there. And hope most people aren't paying attention to what's really happening."

Maya stared at the contract page still in Ted's hand.

"I guess what I don't understand is how our elected officials convince themselves this is actually good for us. Do you think they really believe it?" she asked.

"Maya, do you have a whiteboard?" Ted asked. "This is worth illustrating."

Maya exited to her bedroom, which doubled as her office. She returned with a whiteboard and a couple markers.

Ted propped the whiteboard on her sofa and picked up a marker. He drew a circle in the center and wrote "DATA CENTER" inside it, with arrows radiating outwards.

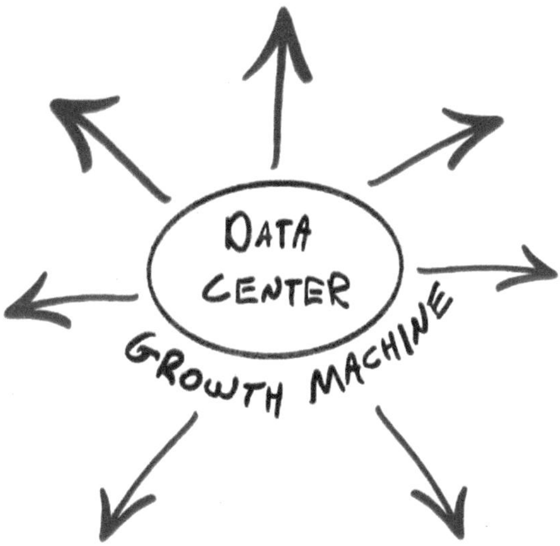

"Researchers who study economic development call this a growth machine." He labeled the arrows as he spoke:

Developers - Commercial real estate - The power company - Banks - Construction companies - Elected officials who want ribbon cuttings - Staff who need wins

He capped the marker and turned to face them. "They all profit from intensive land use. The deals get framed as community benefit but look at who actually makes money."

Harold sat back and looked at the board. "Not one of those arrows points to the community," he said.

The Utility Game

No one had anything to add. Harold pulled the second stack toward him.

"I want to go back to the profit motive," Harold said.

He reached into his nylon briefcase and set his legal pad flat on the table.

"Do you know how utilities actually make their money?"

Maya shook her head.

"Infrastructure. When they build power plants and transmission lines, regulators let them charge a guaranteed return on their equity investment. Nine to eleven percent, every year," he said.

Dusty let out a slow breath. "That's way more than inflation."

"Exactly," Harold continued. "So they have a built-in incentive for massive infrastructure upgrades. Especially ones that benefit huge users. Eleven percent profit, hidden in our bills. That's driving rates higher."

Dusty pushed back from her chair. "So we're the ones paying for the upgrades. Ratepayers who live here."

Harold glanced at Ted. The pieces were starting to line up.

Maya had barely touched her tamales. She'd been standing near the window for the last few minutes, arms crossed, listening.

"Let's take five," Dusty said. "Ice cream. I saw some in your freezer, Maya."

"Good idea," Harold said.

In the kitchen, Harold and Ted scooped generous bowls and headed back to the table.

Maya stood by the counter, arms still crossed. Dusty filled a bowl and pressed it into her hands without a word.

Smokestack Chasing

When they settled back in, Ted picked up the marker.

"This is nothing new. It all lines up. Smokestack chasing. Governments and power companies have always needed each other. Harold just showed you the profit motive. Let me show you how old the playbook is."

He sketched out four dates on the whiteboard, capped the marker, and turned to face them.

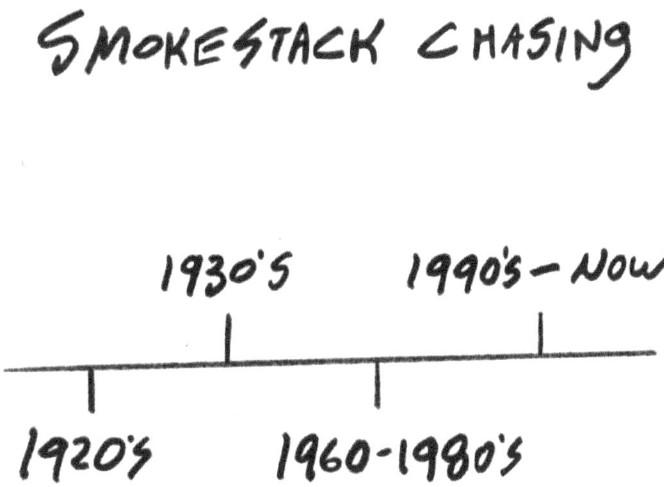

"This all began with Samuel Insull," he said, pointing to the *1920s*.

"He built an empire promising cities cheap electricity in exchange for exclusive franchises. He used the monopoly to decide which neighborhoods got power and which stayed in the dark. Nine out of ten rural families had no electricity at all."

"Wow. Nine out of ten," Harold said.

"Roosevelt broke up the empire," Ted said, tapping on *1930s* with the marker.

"He created federal loans for coops to serve rural people. The utilities called it socialism. The bargain was supposed to protect consumers. But electric needs kept growing, and the power companies moved back in."

He tapped on the third set of dates. "The 60s through the 80s brought tax breaks, infrastructure deals, financial packages, led by power companies with local governments. A new industry popped up marrying those two: dedicated economic development staff, site selection assistance, incentive rates for big industrial customers. All under the guise of job creation."

He moved to the *1990s-Now*.

"And then Congress restructured the whole industry in 1992. Generation became competitive but transmission and distribution stayed monopolies. Utilities kept control of the wires."

"And that matters because...?" Harold asked.

Once Congress finished dismantling the old ownership rules in the early 2000s, foreign companies moved in fast. They've been acquiring American utilities ever since. The profits leave the country."

Maya looked at Dusty. Dusty looked at Ted.

"Co-ops aren't much better. They now can build nine, ten percent profit into the rates on deals like this. It's not on anyone's bill. Members have no idea."

"So rates are skyrocketing everywhere," Dusty said. "Beyond our control."

Maya had stopped following the whiteboard.

It made sense now: the development authority's sudden interest in their work, the vague emails about optimization opportunities, the revelation about the data farm and power deal and now Sarah's silence. They'd wanted her data and her credibility. The real table had always been somewhere else.

She'd thought she had a seat at the table. Now she understood there was another one.

"This is damning," Maya said, her voice flat.

She looked at the whiteboard, then at the three of them.

"So governments chase the deals, utilities build the infrastructure, everyone claims they're creating jobs," she said. "Ratepayers fund it. The development authority gets their money and acts like they're doing us a favor."

She paused. "It's what started a hundred years ago, smokestack chasing. Except now, much of the profit leaves the country. And groups like ours?"

She let that hang for a second. "We're just cover."

"What a con," Dusty sighed.

Pause

Maya cleared her throat. The heat was creeping up her neck. It wasn't anger exactly. It was closer to humiliation.

"There's something I also need to show you," she said.

She walked into her office and came back with a stack of papers. It was a copy of an email, subject line: *Desert Corridor Initiative: Next Steps Discussion.*

She passed it around.

"Someone copied me on this, I think by accident about a month ago. Back when things still felt like they were going somewhere. I didn't think anything of it until yesterday," Maya said.

She read it aloud, her voice catching slightly.

Dusty caught her gaze. "Maya, they've been stringing you along. You've given everything while they fed you nothing but breadcrumbs."

Maya hadn't realized until now just how tight her jaw was and how she'd been clenching her hands.

She took a breath and explained how she'd shared beta data sets and intellectual property covering hundreds of miles of wildlife corridor.

“I thought,” her voice cracked slightly, “I thought Sarah was keeping me in the loop because we were partners, friends even. I gave her what she asked for.”

The room was quiet.

“I need to ask something I'm embarrassed to say out loud.” She forced herself to meet their eyes. “Is it possible they took what I shared and just used us?”

Ted was calm. “That's a pretty good theory,” he said.

“So?” Maya's voice was tight.

Ted's voice was quiet but certain. “All of it is exactly what the people behind these deals need. Wildlife tracking for transmission line placement. Watershed data for permit applications. Water usage documentation for the data farm. Your work could save them millions in environmental consulting fees alone.”

Dusty looked at Maya directly. “That's probably why Sarah kept asking for data updates, screenshots, reports. And why she stopped returning your calls.”

“ But I think she was caught in the middle,” Ted said. “She was probably a true believer, but then somewhere got stuck in the machinery, protecting deals she couldn't talk about.”

“But that doesn’t explain it all,” Maya said. “She could have warned us.”

"Maybe. Unless she was implicated," Ted noted.

Maya looked down. "So they're going to try to use our work to permit the very projects that will destroy the watershed."

"That's the risk," Harold said. "All we have is an MOU. No contract. And Tres Valles rushed that timeline. Our data isn't necessarily protected if the partnership dissolved."

Maya's face burned.

"I shouldn't have shared," Maya said quietly. "I thought her behavior was off because she was stressed about Luke."

No one said anything. Maya pushed back her chair and walked out of the room.

She was gone maybe two minutes. When she came back she was carrying wine glasses and the Chardonnay. She'd already poured herself a large one.

Self-Interest

"I want to encourage you, Maya," Ted's voice was again gentle. "This isn't all on you, it's on all of us. You weren't wrong to trust Sarah. The partners who'd worked with her before trusted her too."

Maya scanned the room. Dusty's face was full of compassion and she was nodding her head in agreement.

"But...we still need a plan to figure out how to pull our work back...that is, if we can," Harold said.

"Yes," Ted agreed. "And before we dive into battle mode, we need to understand motives and what they actually need."

"What do you mean?" Maya asked.

"We need to map out everyone's self-interest," Ted said, uncapping the marker. "That's how we figure out what leverage we might have."

Ted quickly erased the whiteboard and wrote:

SELF INTEREST

"There's a quote I always come back to," Ted said. "Milton Friedman, Nobel Prize winning economist. I don't agree with everything he stood for, but this one stuck with me."

He recited it from memory:

Self-interest is not myopic selfishness. It is whatever it is that interests the participants, whatever they value, whatever goals they pursue.

The scientist seeking to advance the frontiers of his discipline, the missionary seeking to convert infidels to the true faith, the philanthropist seeking to bring comfort to the needy - all are pursuing their interests, as they see them, as they judge them by their own values.

Ted continued. "People and institutions act from self-interest. That's not bad. That's human nature. The problem is when those interests are hidden and people realize too late that someone else's agenda was running the show."

He drew a simple grid:

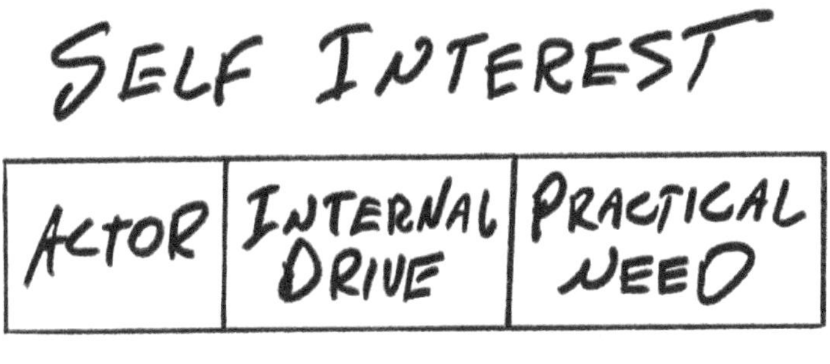

“Self-interest runs on two tracks,” Ted said. “Internal drives, things like feeling valued, belonging to something meaningful, believing in your work. And practical needs, money, promotions, reputation, political wins, shareholder returns. Both are real. Both apply here.”

“So let’s think. Who’s all involved here?” he said.

Ted leaned over and took Harold's legal pad. Harold raised an eyebrow but didn't object.

Ted drew a quick grid. “Government, Tres Valles,” he said, writing it in the first column. “Who else?”

Maya raised her hand. “Those huge data farms.”

“Who else?” Ted said. “Take a look at those arrows I drew.”

“The power company makes a lot of money,” Harold replied. “And real estate interests like leasing companies, developers.”

They worked through it together, calling out actors while Ted filled in the grid. By the time they'd finished, the picture was bigger than tax revenue and profits. It captured reputations, legacies, careers and political futures.

Ted looked down at the grid. He took a photo and sent it to their group chat.

Phones buzzed around the table.

"Okay," he said, glancing down at his own copy.

SELF INTEREST

ACTOR	INTERNAL DRIVE	PRACTICAL NEED
Development Authority	Respect and trust of community	Career advancement for staff and electeds; re-election; tax revenue; economic growth
Power Company (Foreign-owned utility and local staff)	Sense of purpose helping communities; professional identity as job creators	Guaranteed returns (9-11% on infrastructure); shareholder dividends; career advancement
Real Estate & Development Interests	Pride in building legacy projects; vision of regional growth	Development fees + property management income from land value appreciation
Data Farm	Enabling the future AI/cloud economy	Lower taxes; subsidized infrastructure; cheap land; maximum profit

"Let's think about how these interests play out for a moment," he said. "If they try to take our intellectual property, they won't look great if we expose them, will they?"

"What do you mean?" Maya asked.

"Tres Valles and real estate interests and local power company staff want to preserve their respect and the trust of the community, right? They need that to continue working here because they live here," Ted said.

"They won't look good if they're outed as trying to steal our work."

"That's like ranching," Dusty said, "We'd call that knowing who you'll face at the feed store on Monday. The power company and data farm executives are in and out of here. These people live here. That's different."

The Battle Plan

"So what's next?" Harold asked after a long silence. "I think we need a lawyer. Someone who can make them take us seriously. Though the MOU doesn't cover intellectual property. We don't have a clean legal argument."

He shuffled through a few pages he'd pulled from the pile.

"But these emails between the development authority and the power company...if they were using public staff time and public office infrastructure to coordinate messaging that benefits a private company, that's not just bad optics. That's potentially a misuse of public funds. An auditor would flag this. A state ethics board might too."

Maya moved to the window. "We have evidence of collusion. Coordinated messaging, and an email implying they're probably after our IP." She turned back. "It's not definitive. But it's enough."

She paused and picked up her phone.

"And look at Ted's self-interest map. The people most exposed here are the ones who live in this community. The elected officials, the local real estate interests, the development authority staff. They need the community's trust to keep working here. The power company and the data farm can walk away."

Harold set his pen down. "That's the pressure point."

"Definitely leverage," Dusty said. "We tell them we have a story and we're willing to tell it."

Ted looked at Maya. "These are people with a lot of money and power."

"I know," she said. "I'll get my laptop. Let's draft a press release."

An hour later, they had a statement. The others gathered their things and headed out into the night.

Maya read it through one more time. She'd send it in the morning.

Part 4

Rebuilding

Calling It Out

Maya was up early after a night of broken sleep. Coffee in hand, she sat there rebuilding the nerve she had yesterday.

She'd given her heart and soul to this work and to the relationships she'd built over many months. Now she could see it clearly: Sarah had designed the table and assigned every seat. The setting had been impressive, with printed agendas, task lists and even the round table. It looked like partnership. It was hierarchy. When more powerful actors showed interest, the coalition's seats simply disappeared.

Why hadn't she seen this sooner?

She'd been grateful, hopeful and flattered to be seen. She'd missed every sign. This table wasn't real. It was a placeholder for something better that came along.

That clarity was enough. Maya opened her laptop, pulled up the draft email and hit send.

Headline News

The Tres Valles Regional Development Authority's reply came exactly one week later. It followed the morning's news: *Public Trust for Sale: Inside the Data Center Deal.*

The local journalist had nailed it: public records requests, in-depth interviews and enough documentation to make denial impossible. The power company, the hyperscale data farm and local electeds had colluded, and there was more.

Maya was shocked to read that Sarah, along with a handful of Tres Valles staff, had also been doing contract work for a data farm in a neighboring county. According to the press sources, they'd been hired to help obtain permits.

It didn't add up. Why? How could Sarah take that job, working against everything she professed she believed?

Then Maya remembered Sarah's son. Months ago, Sarah had shared about the mounting medical bills she couldn't afford. She must have been caught between her values and survival.

Self-interest, Maya thought. Ted was probably right.

Reply

Her phone buzzed. It was an email from the development authority attorney's office.

Subject: Termination of Partnership MOU

She read it once and then again, slower.

Dear Partners,

After careful consideration, the Tres Valles Regional Development Authority has decided to discontinue the Desert Corridor Partnership effective immediately. Budget constraints require us to focus resources on other priorities. Each party retains full ownership and control of any materials, data and intellectual property provided during the course of this partnership. We appreciate your contributions and wish you well in your future endeavors.

Sincerely,
Attorney's Office
Tres Valles Regional Development Authority

Overwhelmed by relief tangled with uncertainty, Maya forwarded the email to her board and picked up her phone to follow up with calls, hoping to confirm this was good news.

Dusty and Ted seemed to agree their strategy had worked. What they had brought to the partnership still appeared rightfully theirs.

She made her last call, this one to Harold. Unlike Dusty and Ted, he was wary.

"The attorneys might still be using what you put together, Maya, and we'll never really know," Harold said. "But we can try to move forward with what we have."

Her phone buzzed again, more texts coming in rapid succession. She'd already brought Carmen, Terrence and Marcus up to speed on Ted's freedom of information request on a text chain about the closed-door meetings and the deal.

From Marcus: Did you see the headlines???

From Terrence: What the hell is this?! Sarah? And Tres Valles just ended our partnership?!

And a private text from Carmen: CALL ME NOW

Aftermath

Maya called Carmen.

"Did you see this morning's paper?" Carmen opened. "I can't believe it. We were railroaded."

She continued, words pouring out.

"Not even a conversation. We're just dismissed after all that empty talk about partnership."

Maya let her keep going. They agreed to regroup and salvage what they could.

Staying present and steady for the rest of her calls took all Maya's remaining energy. Marcus was furious about the wasted time and resources. Terrence kept circling back to how they should have seen the signs earlier.

At the end of it, Maya crashed on the sofa, still in her pajamas, bone tired.

Stalled

Two weeks later, the partners reconvened around Maya's kitchen table.

By now, they'd absorbed another news story. Details kept trickling in about the data farm deal. Whatever the development authority had been preparing to approve that week was now postponed 'pending further review,' according to a Tres Valles spokeswoman.

Carmen wanted to lead this meeting.

“We’re not letting them do this again,” Carmen opened angrily.

Terrence was calmer, although he chose his words carefully.

“This *is* terrible,” he said. “And I need to understand what we still have together.”

They shared notes about how their boards had reacted. Terrence tried more than once to pull them back to his question. Carmen kept interrupting with grievances.

“They lied to us from day one,” she said.

“We were promised an equal partnership. What a sham!”

"They pulled the rug out once big money was on the table. Complete betrayal."

Marcus was completely shut down.

Terrence reached into his backpack and pulled out a legal pad. He sketched out three columns with their organizations' names across the top and flipped it to show them.

"What is still ours here? What do we have together?" He tapped the paper. "Just us, no Tres Valles?"

Maya surprised herself by answering first. "Data systems. Mapping. And we know how to document things."

Carmen's jaw tightened but she nodded. "Regulatory knowledge. Relationships with landowners."

Terrence filled in his own column: "Youth programs. Volunteers we've trained."

Marcus remained watchful and silent. When he finally spoke, it stopped the room.

"How do we know this won't happen again? And how do we know one of us won't sell out when the pressure is on?"

The room went quiet. Each was thinking about the same thing: the people they'd have to face.

"Building, what each of us has done, that's taken years," Terrence said quietly. "The youth I work with and their families, they're going to ask me what happened. What do I tell them?"

"I don't know..." Carmen said. "And that's what makes me so angry."

There weren't enough words in the room for what they'd lost.

Terrence broke the silence. "We can stay angry. But we also need to survive. I have bills to pay."

Carmen picked up her phone. "I've been thinking the same, Terrence. I've been looking at this small rural development opportunity. It's not enough to scale our work but it might help us keep the lights on."

Maya leaned forward. "Tell us more."

"Federal money," Carmen said. "It's a small grant and requires partnerships. We could work together."

Marcus said nothing. He just looked at the phone.

Terrence tapped the legal pad. "So what does working together actually look like?"

Carmen looked at Marcus, then Terrence, then Maya. "I don't know yet. I think we have to figure that out together."

Noticing: Below the Line

That afternoon, Maya texted her executive committee: *We've got a problem. Our partners are stuck. We met and everyone is frustrated. I need help thinking this through.*

Two days later, Ted, Harold and Dusty were in her living room.

"Our last coalition meeting was depressing," Maya opened. "The table was rigged from the start. It's hard to know how to trust each other enough to move forward."

She laid out what they'd tried to do, but how the anger, Marcus going silent and the questions no one could answer had gotten in the way.

Harold was the first to speak.

"That's to be expected," he sympathized. "What you went through was a blindside, and a really painful one."

Dusty agreed. "You're expressing righteous anger. That's good. Without it, I might doubt your commitment, Maya. And beneath all those feelings, and the anger, is fear."

"Fear?" Maya asked.

"It's fear, and that can keep you looping in circles. I've been there," Dusty said. "Let me show you something," she continued. "Do you have something I can write on?"

Maya left and returned from her office with the whiteboard.

Dusty was ready, sleeves rolled to her elbows. She drew a triangle and labeled the three points:

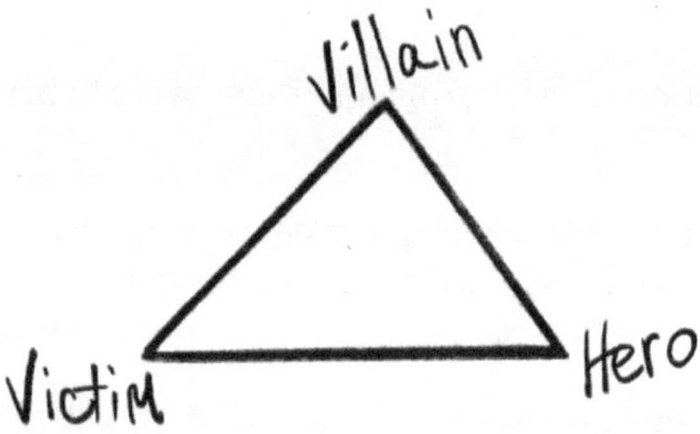

"You see this?" Dusty asked, tracing the triangle. "There's a frame I learned a while back. When you're hurt or threatened, you fall into one of these three. Victim, villain, hero. Every time."

"The villain persecutes. The victim is persecuted. And the hero swoops in to rescue the victim. Sounds noble, but the hero actually keeps everyone stuck. Your group is drowning because everyone's afraid. And it's changing how you see yourselves and each other."

Maya stood up, walked to the whiteboard and studied the triangle.

"I can see all three," she said. "The development authority is the villain, they used us. We're the victims. And though I'm exhausted, part of me wants to be the hero who saves us."

Dusty drew a line above the triangle. She then drew another triangle above the line and labeled the three points:

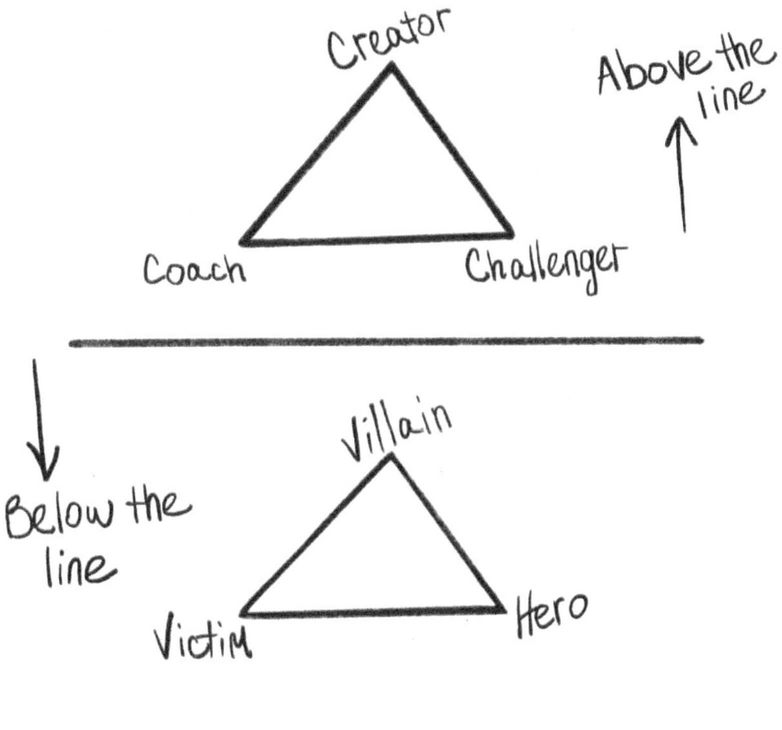

"Get above your fear and everything shifts. You start creating instead of reacting. Coaching instead of rescuing. Challenging instead of blaming."

She tapped the board with her marker. "Brené Brown talks about this. It stuck with me."

"Below this line, you're running on fear, anger, shame. Fight or flight. The thinking brain checks out." She paused. "Above it, you still feel all that but you just notice it before it runs you."

"So how do you get there?" Harold asked.

"You can't push your way up." Dusty said. "You need space. Could be fifteen minutes. Could be weeks. I've learned it the hard way with a couple of ranchers who couldn't get out of their own way."

Maya looked at the triangles. "So right now, we're below the line."

"Probably," Dusty said.

"So we need time," Maya said.

Taking Space

That afternoon, Maya texted the coalition: *Still processing. Let's reconvene in a month.*

Marcus responded first to Maya privately: *I need to step back from the coalition.*

Maya called Marcus.

"I'm afraid I'm holding you all back," Marcus said. "Every time we talk about moving forward, I get stuck."

Maya almost stepped in to reassure him but realized he wasn't finished.

"I still have to file reimbursements with the development authority for our other work. Every time I do it, I'm reminded of what they did to us."

"Yes," Maya said quietly.

Marcus continued. "And honestly? It's too much. Tracking everything, documenting it all, and then doing all this with a group. I don't have bandwidth for that. Neither does my board. We're stretched thin."

"I get it," Maya said. "You've shown up, told us the truth, been a real partner. That matters. And if you can't move forward right now, it's better to say so than to push through something that isn't there."

"Thank you," Marcus said, relief in his voice.

After he hung up, she texted the others: *Marcus is stepping back. We're still on for the 15th.*

Over the next weeks, Maya noticed when she was below the line.

When a neighboring rancher asked what happened, she took a deep breath. She caught herself before blurting out her first thought: *They betrayed us!* Villain language was still nearly a reflex.

She named it in her head: I'm below the line. I'm angry and that's okay.

She kept her reply simple. "It didn't work out. We're figuring out the next steps."

Terrence called a couple days later to talk.

"I don't know if I'm ready," Terrence said. "I can't afford to pour into something that falls apart again."

"I keep hitting walls when I try to think it through," Maya said. "I think we need help. Are you with me on that?"

"Yeah," Terrence said. "I am."

Margaret Arrives

A few weeks later, they gathered in Maya's living room. Ted had suggested keeping it small, with just the partners and Maya's executive committee, until they had something worth bringing to their full boards.

The doorbell rang. Ted was fast on his feet and got the door.

"Come on in," he said, stepping aside. "Everyone, this is Margaret."

Margaret smiled gently. Her silver hair was cropped short and she wore a quilted vest with a faded National Parks Service emblem. She had the calm presence of someone who'd survived decades in bureaucracy and still believed in her work.

At the doorway, she paused to swap her hiking boots for a pair of flats before she settled into a chair.

"I'm sorry I'm late. I was following the cottonwoods," she said. "Then some cattle crossed the road, and when I got back in my car I had to wait for them."

She noticed the whiteboard with the triangles on the sofa. "What's the framework?"

"Dusty outlined it for us a few weeks back," Maya said. "It's helped us name things we couldn't name before."

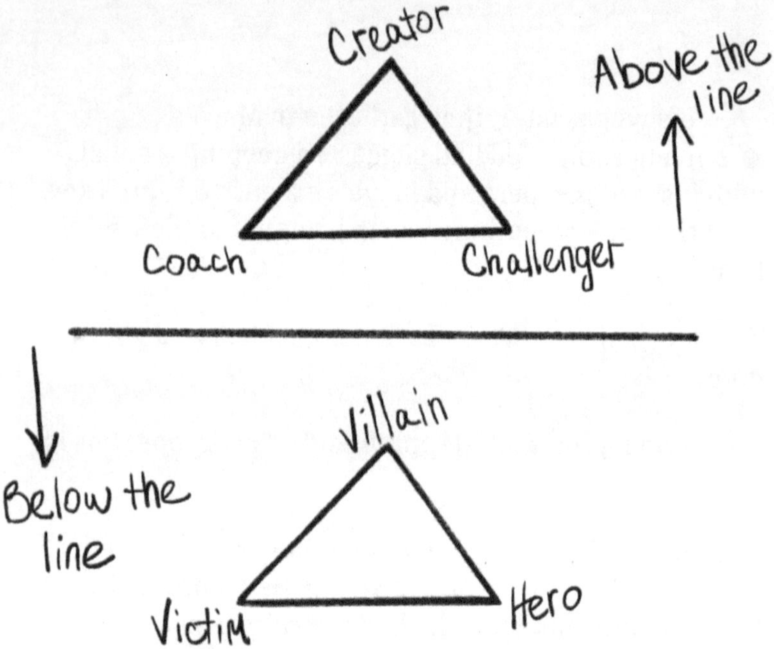

"Show me," Margaret said.

Maya walked her through it. "What's helped me most is realizing I don't have to be above the line to keep going. I can name where I am and still show up."

Margaret nodded, watching her.

"And part of it is being honest about what actually happened." Maya paused. "They didn't just end the partnership. They used us."

"Extracted what they needed," Terrence said.

"Our credibility. Our relationships. The work we'd already done." Maya shook her head. "And then dropped us like we never mattered."

Carmen's voice was flat. "We weren't even tokens. Tokens stay in the jar. They shook us out when they were done with us."

"They made us feel important while we were useful," Maya said. "Sarah would check in, ask good questions, and affirm."

"It feels hard to try to move forward when we aren't past it," Terrence said.

"You're right, you don't have to be past it," Margaret said. "I've never met anyone who was."

The doorbell rang again. It was Dusty. She hung her hat on the hook, work gloves tucked in her back pocket.

"Sorry I'm late. I had to patch a fence section before a calf pushed through it," she said.

She noticed Margaret. "Hi, I'm Dusty. "You must be Ted's expert."

"Mostly trying to retire," Margaret said. "Not quite succeeding. I'm not here to tell you anything you don't already know."

Dusty settled into a chair and glanced at the whiteboard. "I see the triangles came in handy."

“More than you know,” Maya said.

Margaret looked around the room. “Alright. Ted told me you're thinking how you’d all like to move next. Where would you like to start?”

Carmen spoke up. “My board wants to find a convener for this. Someone to coordinate.”

“Let's start there,” Margaret said. “Because I want to push on that a little. A convener can end up doing a lot, guiding vision, managing data, mobilizing funding, controlling communications. That's a lot for one partner. Is that what you want?”

Carmen sat back. “That's exactly what Sarah's office did. We had tasks. They had power. I see that now.”

“Right,” Margaret said. “So what would a real role look like for each of you this time?”

Margaret set up a small projector on Maya's coffee table and connected it to her laptop. The projector hummed to life, throwing a rectangle of light on Maya's wall.

“Carmen, you mentioned a federal funding opportunity,” Margaret said. “Can I see it?”

Carmen had brought hard copies of what she’d already emailed. She passed them around. Margaret scanned quickly.

“Rural development, infrastructure, training funds allowed here.” She looked up. “Let's start simple. What are you trying to do together?”

Tasks List

Margaret typed at the top: **TASKS**

"For this opportunity, what needs to get done?"

Terrence spoke first. "Community outreach. We need to hear from ranchers, small businesses, youth. After this blowup with Tres Valles, we need to go back, listen to them and find out what they actually need."

"Project coordination," Carmen said. "Financial management. Someone has to track the budget, spending, communicate deadlines."

"Data management," Maya said. "Mapping, technical systems. Documentation to prove the model works."

"And youth training," Terrence added. "If we're working with youth, they need to learn these systems too. That creates job skills."

"Sounds like you've already got the pieces to respond to that opportunity," Dusty said. "You just need to put them together."

Ted nodded. "And you built all of this before. Just not together."

Margaret continued to type as they talked.

She produced a clean list on the wall:

TASKS

Community outreach & engagement
Project coordination & fiscal management
Data management & mapping
Youth training in technical systems
Technical documentation

"Good," Margaret said. "Now, who should do this work, and why them?"

"Terrence leaned forward. "You mean it's not just about who's best at the task?"

"Partly," Margaret said. "But the deeper question is: what does each of your organizations actually need from this? Not what sounds good. It's what you truly need to make this worth the risk."

Carmen was quiet for a moment. "That's a harder question."

"Yes," Margaret said.

"We're going to need another board for that," Ted said. He looked at Maya. "The one in your office?"

Maya went to get it.

Self-Interests

Maya handed Ted the whiteboard. He propped it up next to the projected task list.

He uncapped a marker and wrote across the top:

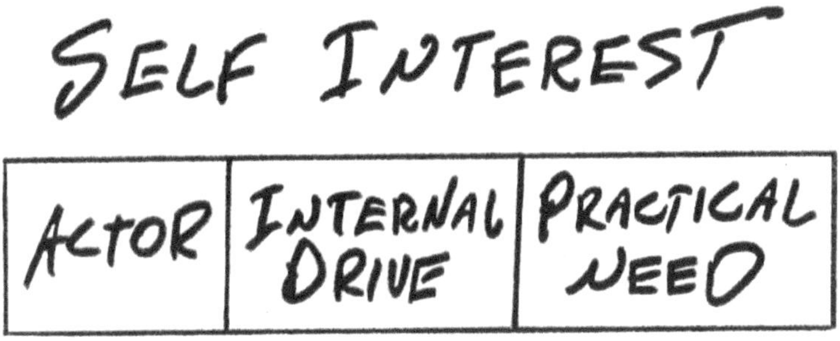

Margaret glanced at Ted. "You mentioned talking about this?"

"Maya and I got into it awhile back," Ted said.

"Good. Then let's be honest," he continued. "What do each of you need from this partnership to make it worth your time and risk? Practically and personally."

He looked around. "And don't be put off by the phrase *self-interest*."

"Self-interests aren't wrong. They're motivators. The problem is when they're hidden."

"Like with Sarah," Maya said quietly.

"So," Margaret said. "What do you need?"

Carmen went first. "My board needs to see results. And fast. They're wondering if partnerships are even worth it after this whole mess."

Carmen set her water bottle down.

"I need to show them something concrete. To show them our organization can lead," Carmen finished.

Terrence spoke next. "Our youth program needs job placements, jobs where they stay employed. Not just training that goes nowhere. And we need to know how much they're earning as they move through those jobs. Without that, we lose funding."

Maya was next. "We need to prove this restoration model works. If we can show it with data, that opens funding for the whole region."

Ted filled in the board as they spoke, short phrases in each column. Margaret studied it and was typing along on her laptop.

"I'm capturing this into something we can share and come back to."

She projected the cleaned-up version next to Ted's board:

TABLE 2: SELF-INTEREST

ACTOR	INTERNAL DRIVE	PRACTICAL NEED
Maya's Wildlife Corridor	Prove model; technical excellence	Documentation opens funding
Carmen's Land Trust	Show board partnerships; restore credibility	Concrete results fast; leadership
Terrence's Youth Services	Build trust with local youth	Job placements; maintain funding

Matching Tasks to Interests

Margaret pulled up a blank grid on the projector, tasks on one side, their organizations across the top.

"I'll type," she said. "You tell me where each task lands and why it serves your organization."

It went fast. Carmen took project coordination and fiscal management, tasks her board would recognize as leadership. Maya took data management and mapping, evidence that affirmed her expertise and opened doors to funding. Terrence took youth training. Paired with Maya's data collection, he believed it could show earnings with real complementary data.

"See what you've done?" Margaret said. "Every task is doing double duty. The work itself meets your needs. That's when people stay invested."

Carmen studied the projection. "So when I'm managing the budget, I'm not just doing it for the project. I'm doing it because my board needs to see me leading."

"Exactly," Margaret said. "When that's clear, you show up differently. You're invested because it serves your actual needs."

"Needs for now," Ted cautioned. "But these can change."

"They can and do. That's why you should capture them now," Margaret said.

She paused. "And they're shaped by people who aren't even in the room. That's your boards, your volunteers, your clients. Partnerships fail when the work stops serving people's actual interests. You come back, map them again, adjust."

Terrence sat back. "So the people out of the room matter as much as the ones in it."

"Sometimes more," Margaret said.

Dusty crossed her arms. "So we've been doing this backwards the whole time."

"Most people do," Margaret said. "Matching tasks to interests is your first protection. If interests don't align, don't force the partnership."

She clicked to a new slide. "But you're also building something together. And that means sharing the decisions, the work, the care for it."

Common Goals

Maya looked at the screen. "I thought that's what we just did. Who does what," she said.

"That's task distribution," Margaret said. "Important. But I want to talk now about common goals. What you're building together, not just who's doing which piece. That's the step that builds on this."

She projected a new table:

TASKS VS. COMMON GOALS

TASKS	COMMON GOALS
Serve individual interests Each person does their part	Requires building together Distributes: • POWER: Who decides? • AUTHORITY: Who can question and act? • RESPONSIBILITY: Who does work?

"Tasks serve individual interests. You each do your part," she said.

"Getting to common goals requires something harder. Distributing not just the work, but the power to decide, the authority to question and to act."

Ted broke in.

"Tres Valles had power and authority. We just had the responsibility. That's why one email could end everything. This time we share all three from the start."

"That's it," Margaret said. "So let's start with common goals. To go after this funding, what do you need to build together that none of you could build alone?"

Maya spoke first. "We all need to learn federal compliance. Carmen and Terrence have used federal funds before. But I haven't."

"Good," Margaret said, typing. "What else?"

"Communication standards," Terrence said. "We all need to respond reliably. Not like..." he trailed off.

"Breadcrumbing," Ted finished.

"Yes," Margaret said. "What else?"

"Budget transparency," Carmen said, her words coming with effort. "If we're going to share power, we all need to see the books. All of us need to be able to question how money is spent."

"And decisions," Maya added. "A process where we all have a say."

"What about the data systems?" Margaret asked.

"We all need to contribute evidence," Maya said, "Evidence that's accessible to everyone."

Margaret had been typing as they talked. She projected another table:

COMMON GOALS

WHAT WE'RE BUILDING TOGETHER	WHO DOES WHAT
Learn federal compliance together	Each leads one section, teaches others
Communicate reliably	All commit to standard
Share budget openly with all partners	Carmen as fiscal agent, opens books quarterly
Make decisions together	Maya designs process; Terrence docs; Carmen checks
Prove model works with data	All contribute evidence; Maya synthesizes & safeguards

Carmen suggested adjusting the communication goal to be more specific, a 48 hour turnaround. Maya tweaked the language on decision-making to include consensus.

“This makes sense,” Maya said.

Margaret made the adjustments.

“Carmen and Terrence, you said you've used federal money before, right?” she asked.

They both nodded.

“We need to talk about compliance next,” Margaret said.

Compliance

Margaret scanned the room. It was quiet. She walked to the whiteboard, erased Ted's scrawl, and wrote one word:

COMPLIANCE

“I'm guessing that word makes you nervous,” she said.

Terrence laughed uncomfortably. “A little. I’ve always hated it, especially when our federal grants officer brings it up.”

“We've both managed federal grants,” Carmen clarified. “Small ones. Honestly, I'm always worried we're going to get audited and they'll find we did something wrong.”

“We're under the audit threshold though,” Terrence added. “So that won't happen.”

“Maybe, maybe not,” Margaret said. “You can still get audited by the federal agency no matter the size of your grant. And auditors look for more than most organizations realize.”

Terrence and Carmen exchanged glances.

Harold looked up from his notepad, reading glasses still on his nose. “Not having systems kills nonprofits,” he said.

He clicked his mechanical pencil. “I worked with one in Cleveland that shut down over a $15,000 audit finding. The director spent the money right. He just couldn't prove it.”

“And it’s not just the money,” Margaret said. “Conflicts of interest policies, procurement policies, clear internal controls. All are required. Most groups think they'll just build the plane while flying it.”

“That's exactly what it feels like most of the time,” Carmen admitted. “Flying blind.”

Margaret wrote on the whiteboard:

> COMPLIANCE =
>
> SOMEONE DOING WHAT THEY SAY THEY'LL DO TO A CERTAIN STANDARD

"That's what compliance means," she said. "You say you'll spend money on supplies? Show the timestamped receipts and approvals. You say partners will review the budget quarterly? Show the documentation it happened."

Maya looked up. "So the receipts, the approvals. That's not just paperwork. That's the proof."

"Right," Margaret said. "And there's a framework for all of it, Uniform Guidance, 2 CFR Part 200."

She paused.

"The policies you need, what records to keep, how to make spending decisions, how to prove you did it right. Most of it is common sense once you understand the why behind it," she said.

Terrence rubbed the back of his neck. "Honestly, we've been spending federal money without really understanding all that. We're trying, but it's hard."

"That's more common than you think," Margaret said. "And it's fixable.

She reached for her laptop.

"Let me show you something first," she said. "A little context helps."

She projected an image on the wall. "This is the Fuggerei, in Augsburg, Germany. Built in 1521."

She clicked to the next photo, displaying rows of modest, well-kept houses behind a vine-covered gated wall.

“Humans have been figuring out how to formalize trust for centuries.”

She turned to face them.

“European merchants in the Middle Ages had no central government to enforce contracts. So guilds did it themselves. If a merchant didn't pay his debts, every member of his guild could be held liable. In a foreign port, their goods could be seized to cover the bad debt. Then they'd go home and seek compensation from the original defaulter.”

“So they had skin in each other's game,” Carmen said.

“That’s what made them vulnerable to one another’s failures. It created strong incentive to help each other succeed and catch problems early.”

“That sounds terrifying,” Maya said.

“It was. But guilds also protected their members fiercely. Kings wanted to seize money from foreign merchants who were easy targets. Guilds threatened to boycott kingdoms that tried. And no trade meant no tariff revenue. That kept most rulers in check.”

Dusty spoke up. “That's like cattle associations. We’re all in on the brand inspection system. If one rancher doesn't follow protocol, it puts all herds at risk for disease or theft. We watch over each other.”

“That's right,” Margaret said. “Same principles, and here's what they did.”

She turned back to the photos. "Jakob Fugger was a wealthy guild merchant. He took everything here, the guild record-keeping, the mutual accountability, the shared liability, and built this. Social housing in Augsburg. One hundred and fifty people still live there today, five hundred years later."

"Five hundred years?" Carmen asked.

Margaret nodded. "Not government-run. Owned and managed by the community itself. Fugger applied those same guild principles. Kept records of everything, tracked who needed help, made decisions together about who could live there and under what conditions."

"But why?" Terrence asked. "Why would a wealthy merchant do that?"

"Guild values," Margaret said. "They were about the common good. Members helped each other in times of need, cared for widows and orphans. The Fuggerei was an extension of that."

She reached for her water bottle and took a long drink, then looked at each of them.

"You three are doing something similar. You're building structures that serve your individual interests, yes. And also building on shared values, protecting the watershed, creating opportunities for youth, preserving ranching."

"And those values," Margaret paused, "need compliance checks to prove you meant them."

Carmen tapped her pen on the table. “So it's not just following rules. It's about making our values real through systems that prove we mean what we say.”

“Yes,” Margaret said. “That's exactly it.”

“If you really want to build trust, carry it like the guilds did,” she said. “Measure progress against an agreed standard, with evidence everyone can see.”

Margaret projected a third column, each row tagged with a citation.

“I pulled these before I drove up. Now I'm just lining them up with what you've decided.”

COMMON GOALS + COMPLIANCE

WHAT WE'RE BUILDING TOGETHER	WHO DOES WHAT	UNIFORM REQUIREMENTS 2 CFR Part 200
Learn federal compliance together	Each leads one section, teaches others	2CFR Part 200
Communicate reliably within 48 hrs	All commit to standard	200.332 Subaward monitoring
Share budget openly with all partners	Carmen as fiscal agent, open books quarterly	200.302 Financial management
Make decisions by consensus	Maya designs process; Terrence docs; Carmen checks	200.318(c) Procurement conflicts of interest 200.112 Conflict of interest
Prove model works with data	All contribute evidence; Maya synthesizes & safeguards; partners define success metrics	200.301 Performance measurement 200.329 Monitoring and reporting performance

Maya hesitated. "I'm going to ask really basic questions."

Carmen looked at her. “Like what?”

“2 CFR Part 200. What does that stand for?” Maya asked.

“My mistake, I should have provided more context,” Margaret said. “That’s just the legal framework governing federal funds. And Maya, that's exactly the right thing to do, ask questions. Lots of them.”

Carmen stared at the table. “This is a lot.”

“It is,” Margaret agreed. “And it is your foundation.”

“Doing this together means more meetings,” Terrence said. “More coordination.”

“It does,” Margaret agreed. “But it also means if one of you gets stuck, the other two can help. If one of you makes a mistake, the other two catch it. And if you build this right, you'll have systems that outlast any of you.”

Carmen and Maya looked at each other.

“Alright,” Terrence said. “Let's try it.”

Gratitude

Margaret turned back to the group.

"There's one more piece," she said. "Gratitude."

She went back to the whiteboard and erased it again. She drew:

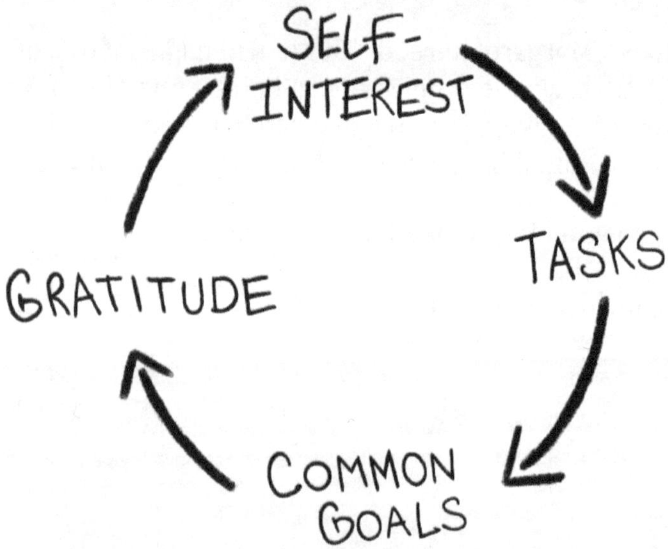

"You name specific recognition for what someone did. That's how you build gratitude among people who've shared power and proven it."

"Proven how?" Maya pressed.

"Evidence," Carmen said. "If I say I'm opening the books quarterly and I actually do it, and you review them and ask real questions, that's documented. It happened."

"And it's something you did together," Margaret said. "Gratitude becomes reciprocal. You give. You receive. You prove it with compliance. Then you acknowledge it specifically."

"Let's go through it," Margaret said. "Starting with learning compliance together. How do you acknowledge that?"

Harold wanted a potluck with all the boards. Maya was excited about hosting a quarterly coffee when they actually hit the communication standard.

Carmen wanted to put budget transparency in Terrence's newsletter, something Terrence said would make his funders happy.

All of them would name the consensus process in their grant reporting.

Margaret was typing quickly, then produced the completed table:

Common Goals → Compliance → Gratitude

WHAT WE'RE BUILDING TOGETHER	WHO DOES WHAT	UNIFORM REQUIREMENTS	GRATITUDE - HOW WE ACKNOWLEDGE
Learn federal compliance together	Each leads one section, teaches others	2CFR Part 200	Potluck party, invite boards to learn together
Communicate reliably within 48 hours	All commit to standard	200.332 Subaward monitoring	Quarterly coffee when we hit standard
Share budget openly with all partners	Carmen as fiscal agent, opens books quarterly	200.302 Financial management	Carmen featured in Terrence's newsletter as model fiscal agent
Make decisions by consensus	Maya designs process; Terrence docs; Carmen checks	200.318(c) Procurement conflicts of interest 200.112 Conflict of interest	Each organization shares process in grant reports
Prove model works with data	All contribute evidence; Maya synthesizes & safeguards; partners define success metrics	200.301 Performance measurement 200.329 Monitoring and reporting performance	All named in data reports to funders

"For each common goal, you map exactly how you'll acknowledge when someone delivers. Not vague thanks. Specific recognition."

Maya studied the column. "What if someone doesn't deliver?"

"The gratitude column stays empty," Margaret said. "And you know there's a problem before you go deeper."

"So it's a warning system," Carmen said.

"A feedback system," Margaret said. "It tells you when trust is building and when it's not."

Terrence nodded. "Good. Before you're in too deep."

"These are really specific," Carmen said.

"They have to be," Margaret said. "Vague thank yous don't build trust. Specific acknowledgments of specific contributions do. You acknowledge people when they've done what they said they'd do, to the standard you agreed on, with evidence everyone can see."

"This feels like it has potential," Terrence said. "I don't trust it yet. It's different."

"Different is what you want," Margaret said. "Trust comes by doing this again, watching each other follow through. You won't necessarily feel it right away."

She looked around the room. "And when things change, you cycle back. You map self-interests. And tasks, common goals, compliance, gratitude. Start over."

"We never thought to map any of this," Carmen said. "Sarah just arranged everything."

"Because it was her table," Margaret said. "She set the terms. You just showed up. This is different. Now it's your table."

Pulling It Together

Dusty had been leaning back in her chair, a boot crossed over her knee.

She stood up and picked up the marker. "Can I put this in a picture? It's how I hold it in my head."

Margaret stepped aside. "Go ahead."

"Maya, you got another board?" Dusty asked.

Maya went down the hall and came back with a smaller one, propping it up next to Ted's. Dusty picked up a marker.

"Maya, I remember when you told us what Sarah said about being trustworthy. Personal trustworthiness matters. But it's not enough." She paused, marker in hand. "What you all built tonight has a shape to it. Let me show you."

She drew a triangle and labeled the points. In the middle she wrote *Reciprocity*.

Terrence caught her eye. "Dusty, I'm noticing a pattern with you and shapes."

"Three points is what people can hold," she said. "Four and you start losing corners."

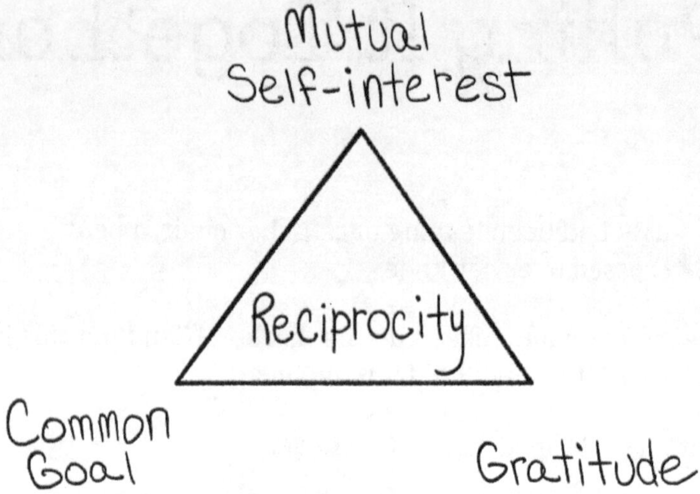

She tapped mutual self-interest. “Not just yours, not just theirs. Everyone names what they need.”

She moved to common goal. “What are we actually doing together? Are we sharing power, authority, responsibility to get there?”

Then she pointed at gratitude. “Do we thank each other? Acknowledge what people bring?”

She stepped back. “And reciprocity, here in the middle, that’s what holds it together.”

Terrence tilted his head. “That triangle, you’re right. It makes sense now.”

Then she drew a rounded line and wrote underneath the whole thing:

"Follow through to shared standards. That's the container," she said. "And that's compliance."

She let it sit for a second.

"People hear compliance and think about paperwork. But here's how you know whether you're doing this right. That's trust."

Margaret was looking at the board, smiling, with her arms crossed, nodding.

"That's what we didn't have before," Maya said. "We had no foundation under any of it."

"No container," Dusty said. "Without it, whoever has the most power tends to set the rules. Compliance levels the ground."

"So what's next?" Carmen asked.

Maya looked at the triangle, then at Margaret's projected table and Ted's self-interest whiteboard.

"The rural development opportunity," she said. "We pursue it. But we write the proposal from this. Not around it."

"And once you're funded," Margaret said, "you go back and assess. Are we doing what we said? What's working? What do we adjust?"

"Documented," Carmen said, reaching for her phone. "That I can sell to my board."

Submitted

Six weeks later, Maya hit 'submit' on the federal grant application.

She texted Carmen and Terrence: *It's done.*

The three of them met at Maya's house that evening, exhausted but lighter.

"We did it," Terrence said, collapsing onto the couch.

"I didn't think we'd get here," Carmen said.

Maya opened a bottle of wine to share. "To possibilities," she toasted them.

Award Notice

A few months later, the email came.

Award Notice: Congratulations!
Your application has been selected for funding.

Maya called Carmen.

"We got it," she said, hardly believing it.

Carmen went quiet for a second, then, "We did it!" Maya heard her telling someone in the background.

She called Terrence next.

"Are you serious?" His voice cracked. "We won?"

"We did."

Back at the Table

Six months later, Maya stood in her kitchen watching trucks pull into her driveway. Carmen was first. Terrence followed.

As they'd been working together, something bigger was taking shape. Ranchers had started calling. Small donors had come forward. People who'd watched the mess unfold with Tres Valles wanted to support what Maya, Carmen and Terrence were building instead.

Carmen came through the door carrying a folder. "Harold reviewed everything but can't make it today."

Terrence arrived grinning. "Seven placements. We projected five."

"Seven?" Maya set down the coffee pot. "How?"

"Feds are funding five. A local construction company picked up two more."

Margaret, Ted and Dusty showed up next. They gathered around Maya's living room table.

"Look at you," Margaret said, scanning their faces. The exhaustion was there, but so was something else.

Dusty settled into a chair. "Ranchers are impressed. I've been hearing about it."

Margaret opened her laptop. "You built something. Now you need to know if it's working."

She looked around the table. "Remember Dusty's triangle? That's what we're checking today. Three questions, one for each corner."

Terrence smiled. "I actually remembered it. Used it with my board too to explain why this partnership was worth it."

"First: mutual self-interest," Margaret said. "Did each of you get what you needed out of this? Not what you said you needed six months ago. What you need now."

"Second: common goals. Did you build what you said you'd build together? And who held the authority when decisions came up?"

"Third: gratitude. Are you still thanking each other? Still naming what people bring? Because that's how people stay."

Margaret turned the laptop toward them and projected onto Maya's wall.

Trust Progress Dashboard - Check-in

Did we each get what we needed? Did we build what we said? Can we prove it?

Triangle check	This Period	Last Period	Evidence
Mutual self-interests met? Can each partner point to concrete benefits?			
Common goals achieved? Did we build what we said? Who had power, responsibility, authority?			
Gratitude flowing? Is recognition happening? What doors opened?			
Compliance as container: Can we prove it? Systems and documentation current?			

Ready for next cycle?

☐ Yes: continue to deeper trust

☐ Not yet: need to address:

____

"Let's talk through it," Ted said.

Carmen went first. "I'm getting what I need. My board has stopped questioning the partnership. Six months of watching us deliver helped. Now they want to know what happens if I ever leave."

She paused. "And I don't want to be the person holding this together forever."

"What would help you get there?" Margaret asked.

"To trust this without constantly looking over my shoulder. I'm not there yet," Carmen said.

No one rushed to fill the space.

Terrence leaned in. "Seven placements. The construction company's interests align perfectly with ours. They want youth with real skills, and the documentation is happening."

Maya went last. "Our data systems work. Next month, youth start training to do analyses themselves. Technical excellence is opening doors."

She hesitated. "But we need better intellectual property agreements before we scale. That's what keeps me up."

Dusty nodded. "You're thinking forward instead of sitting on what you have."

Margaret filled in the dashboard as they talked.

Dusty had been quiet through most of it. She set down her coffee.

“I want to add something,” Dusty said. “We're tracking whether people get what they need. Money, skills, placements. But we're not tracking whether we actually matter to each other.”

The room remained still.

“Belonging and mattering aren't the same thing,” Dusty said. “I picked that up from some reading. You can belong somewhere and still have no idea whether you matter to anyone there.”

“In ranching, your neighbor might let you water your cattle at their tank during a drought if you ask. But you know you matter when they've opened the gate before you got there.”

She looked at the dashboard.

“The development authority let us belong. We had a seat. But we didn't matter to them, not one bit. We can track everything perfectly, check every box. But if people don't feel seen, we're just doing extraction with better paperwork.”

“So what would you add?” Margaret asked.

“Simple questions. Every check in like this we ask: Do you see what’s driving me? When I was here, why did it matter it was specifically me?”

Margaret looked up from her notes. "That's self-interests. Mutual awareness."

"Exactly," Dusty said.

Carmen spoke up. "That's really different than whether we filed reports on time."

"Yep," Dusty said. "Which is probably why most partnerships skip it. Counting tasks is easy. But it's not what keeps people around when the going gets hard."

"What kept me coming back wasn't just the work," Terrence said. "Sure, I wanted to keep our doors open. But it was Maya checking in on me. Carmen too. That's what made me stay."

Maya looked at Margaret. "Can we add that? Not as some warm-fuzzy thing, but as a real question we ask ourselves?"

Margaret was already typing.

"Adding it now," she said. "Mattering check-ins. When people showed up, did it matter that it was specifically them?"

Margaret looked up. "Compliance tells you if the structure's working. This tells you if you're meeting people's needs. Both get you to the next cycle."

Dusty picked up her coffee cup. "And doing it without knowing yet if it'll hold," she said. "That's above the line in real life."

Margaret opened a new row on the dashboard. She turned to the group, “Let's fill in what's changed.”

They went through the rest of it together. Carmen read numbers. Terrence pulled up his phone. Maya flipped through her notebook. Margaret typed as they talked.

When they got to the mattering row, the room slowed down.

Thirty minutes later, the dashboard told their story.

Dusty gave the table a single tap with her knuckles.

“Huh,” she said. “We actually did it.”

What Holds True

A few weeks later, Maya found a package in her mailbox. Inside was a small wooden sign with a note on Dusty's ranch letterhead:

Maya:

Most ranchers I know have some version of this on their wall. Mine's been hanging in my office for twenty years. I thought you'd earned one too. —Dusty

The sign was simple wood with burned lettering:

Stuck to the bottom was a yellow post-it in Dusty's handwriting: *Trust + Verify = Partnership*

Maya turned the sign over in her hands.

She found a perfect spot on her kitchen wall where she'd see it every morning.

That evening, Maya stood at her kitchen window as the sun went down. The cottonwoods down her lane disappeared in the dark, but she knew they were there, roots following the underground streams even in drought.

She looked back at her living room table. A seat at this table was enough.

Part 5: How To Build Trust That Lasts

A note on voice: *I, Angela, wrote these pages, weaving together work from two collaborations. The trust-building framework draws on a decade of research, fieldwork and measurement that Mary Adam, MD, Ph.D. and I built together, validated by collaborators in public health systems (research is referenced at the end of this book). The validation of compliance as a measurable form of trust is new ground in this chapter, developed with Jenni Moreno, whose expertise in federal grants management and compliance practice made that connection possible.*

Building Trust and Your Seat at the Table

Maya's experience will feel familiar if you've spent enough time building partnerships. People care and they show up. They make sacrifices. They push through together, even when it's hard.

Yet, something still often falls apart. We have seen it too.

Sometimes the collapse is dramatic. A powerful partner skims resources for their own priorities. Other times the process is slow and subtle. Early excitement fades or partners disengage.

When things blow up or fizzle out, people wonder: What happened? We shared goals, values, plans and ways we'd get the work done. How did we end up here?

This section helps you diagnose how to build trust or rebuild it when it breaks. Trust is not a given. In partnerships, it is the direct result of creating structures and provable accountability.

Failure isn't typically about bad intentions. Failure results from treating trust as assumed rather than a deliberate practice.

Without intention, unspoken assumptions and expectations can accumulate and often destroy the heart of the work. Trust must be built, tested and repaired in ways that are explicit, shared and measurable.

Building trust requires a different kind of table than the one Maya came to at the beginning, as we show on the following page.

OLD TABLE	NEW TABLE
Beautifully set, impressive, formal	Simple, portable, circular
One actor designed it, assigned seats	Built together, no head
What looked like partnership was actually hierarchy	Power, authority responsibility distributed by design (shared learning)
Real power consolidated behind closed doors	Negotiating happens where everyone can see
When more powerful actors wanted space, community interests were pushed aside	Built to resist capture; can be moved, adjusted, rebuilt as needed

Why We Wrote This Book

We've spent decades in this work, although we arrived in different ways.

I came to it by designing, implementing and evaluating community and economic development programs and partnerships and aligning those to compliance frameworks.

Jenni came to it through her expertise in finance and federal grants management compliance, applying best practices to keep everyone at the table protected and accountable.

Together, we've worked with governments, nonprofits, foundations, public and private sector associations and small businesses. Like you, we seek to build opportunities where those impacted drive the decisions, not just receive them.

I grew up as a child of missionaries in Venezuela and left in my late teens when that government started collapsing. I've spent my career in city planning and community and economic development, building and implementing initiatives aimed at being accountable to the strengths, assets and needs of the people they serve. I'm also a follower of Christ. He believed every person had inherent worth, saw people others overlooked, served them, and then called them to speak, act and build from their own stories. I see this most closely as a parent of an adult child with a disability; alongside others, I'm supporting a network where self-advocates shape what gets built. I don't get it right every time, but I try to follow his example: listening to people the systems overlook and building with them so they can claim their seat at the table.

Jenni came to this work carrying something personal: the memory of watching someone she loves lose everything to systems and people that should have protected her. It stirred in her a passion to ensure people understand where they're operating before those systems are used against them. It taught her that in business you have to be discerning, to stay curious about promises made by those in power, to dig deeper, ask questions and to remember that trust is built, not assumed. Jenni is a connector at heart, and has spent her career building trust across relationships, mentoring young people, coaching small business owners and walking grant recipients through the complexities of federal compliance.

When people understand the rules, who wrote them, and what they agreed to, they can recognize when something is wrong and speak up. That's the work we keep coming back to, even when life tries to pull us away.

What Follows

We write from different contexts and through different lenses. After decades of this work, I have helped coalitions build something greater than any one partner could alone, and watched others collapse when institutions couldn't recognize the people closest to the work were best suited to lead it. Jenni has sat with people and organizations who did everything right and still lost, because the rules that could have protected them were out of reach for the people who needed them most.

What we have both come to believe is this: organizations can do together what no single one can do alone, but only when the work itself is shared in ways accountable to the people they affect. People can sustain hard work and significant challenges when they feel seen for who they are and what drives them, not just for what they deliver.

We start below with a conceptual framework for trust building because it's important to see how trust works before you can protect it.

We follow by showing how unchecked power dynamics undermines shared self-interests, common goals and gratitude.

We end by demonstrating how trust can be measured to a collective standard. That is compliance: following through to standards everyone agreed to, with evidence everyone can see.

Many have experienced compliance as a burden imposed from outside. We see it differently. It is a protective container that makes trust visible to everyone at the table.

Examining trust, power and compliance together reveals what is holding in your partnerships and what needs attention.

1. Framework: Understanding the Three Building Blocks of Trust

Trust is not just a feeling. It is something you can see and measure.

This starts with personal trustworthiness. We want to pause here and recognize Dr. Henry Cloud's excellent work on this topic (referenced at the end of this book), because it shapes how we think about trust. You always need good, trustworthy people to build strong partnerships. At the same time, personal trustworthiness alone is not enough to build organizational trust.

You saw this in the story. Personal trustworthiness couldn't protect Maya's partnership because the structures around it concentrated unchecked power. In the rebuilding, the partners reckoned with how power was held, named their self-interests, identified shared goals and practiced gratitude. Through that, they built trust.

After years of reviewing the research, Dr. Mary Adam, and I reached the clear conclusion that most trust studies either focus on personal characteristics of trustworthiness or they capture trust as a snapshot among actors at static moments in time.

Neither shows how trust actually moves. That is why we developed an alternative conceptual model, grounded in our applied research across community development and health systems. This treats trust as a living process.

Dr. Adam and I found reciprocity drives that movement across three elements that work in concert: self-interests, common goals, and gratitude. The mechanism is simple: when you meet my interests, I want to meet yours; when the cycle stops, trust erodes.

Until now, trust, power and compliance have stayed separate because the people who work in each space rarely share the same table. That separation is what can leave everyone doing this work exposed. Trust researchers don't usually talk to compliance officers. Community organizers working to alter power structures rarely collaborate with grant managers.

We connect them here, and what we have found is that compliance isn't just compatible with trust building. It's one of the missing mechanisms that makes trust measurable. It starts with the three elements that determine whether trust holds or breaks.

Self-Interest: The Fuel for Participation

In the story, you saw how hidden interests derailed the original partnership. Interests, whether disclosed or hidden, drive the work. Ted pointed to Milton Friedman, the Nobel Prize-winning economist, who said it plainly:

Self-interest is not myopic selfishness. It is whatever it is that interests the participants, whatever they value, whatever goals they pursue. The scientist seeking to advance the frontiers of his discipline, the missionary seeking to convert infidels to the true faith, the philanthropist seeking to bring comfort to the needy. All are pursuing their interests, as they see them, as they judge them by their own values.

Elinor Ostrom and Vernon Smith, also Nobel Prize winners, spent their careers proving how people can best work together when cooperation serves their interests. They later collaborated on a volume, *Trust and Reciprocity* connecting their work (shown in our resources section at the end of this book).

As an undergraduate at the University of Arizona, I participated in Vernon Smith's experimental economics lab, where he tested how market structures shape decision making in controlled settings. His work helped establish laboratory experiments as a legitimate tool for studying economic behavior.

What that made me later wonder was: if self-interest drives economic behavior in controlled settings, how does it work in the messy, underfunded partnerships of community development? The answer is the same, but the stakes are different. In a lab, people walk away. In a partnership, they lose funding, relationships and years of work.

Research distinguishes between two types of self-interest that matter in partnerships. Both are legitimate and need to be named:

Internal drives (intrinsic motivation) is what *motivates* you from within: belonging, purpose, the chance to build skills that matter, doing work that aligns with deeply held values, solving problems you care about with people you respect and feeling valued for who you are and what you contribute. Studies show internal drives predict whether people stay engaged when work gets hard, whether they innovate when structures allow it and whether they sustain effort beyond what's required.

Practical needs (extrinsic motivation) include the *realities* we navigate and the *results* we seek from collaborating: resources to keep operations going, reputation that opens doors, network access that creates opportunities, board pressure to show concrete results and funder expectations you must meet for organizational survival. These aren't shallow concerns. They're the reality of organizational work. Ignore them and people burn out.

In the story everyone had self-interests, but not everyone named them and almost no one named both practical needs and internal drives.

The people at the table weren't the only ones with interests at stake. Sarah's boss brokered the out-of-sight, revolving door relationships between government and utilities. Her boss' boss was an elected official making promises to big money behind closed doors.

No one mapped those players' interests in advance. David Lax and James Sebenius's seminal work on three-dimensional negotiation shows the table is only the third dimension. The first two, or setup and scope, are where shadow actors do their work, sometimes deciding the outcome before anyone sits down (see the resources section for more).

These dynamics plays out at every level of a partnership. Individual staff need skill-building and meaningful work. Executive directors need funding for operations and professional credibility. Boards want tangible outcomes. Communities want resources that stay local and serve their priorities. Miss any of these, inside the room or out, and the unmapped interests will likely steer the outcome.

Interests also evolve. What organizations need in year one differs from year three. As partnerships deepen, interests move from surface needs to deeper vulnerabilities. That honesty is itself a sign of trust.

Common Goals: Building Shared Capacity

When the Desert Corridor Partnership began, everyone had a given role. Maya managed technology and data. Carmen worked on landowner relationships. Marcus focused on energy while Terrence worked with youth. Sarah controlled the partners with separate streams of parallel work. When Tres Valles' email ended it all, the coalition had to realign their work to protect it. Divided tasks had kept them efficient, separate and exposed.

Self-interests fuel individual effort. They don't, by themselves, fuel collective benefit.

Elinor Ostrom won the Nobel Prize in Economic Sciences in 2009, and was the first woman to do so, by proving groups can self-govern shared resources without privatization or central regulation. Her research documented how communities managed forests, fisheries and irrigation systems through collective action, not because they were coerced, but because they built structures to share the work and the benefits. She challenged the dominant belief that resources collapse into the 'tragedy of the commons,' where top-down solutions or privatization are inevitable. Ostrom showed a third way: self-organized cooperation can emerge among those who depend on the resource.

What Ostrom's work makes clear is that groups sharing common goals and distributing power can solve problems no single organization can tackle alone. Yet most partnerships treat task completion as the destination, when it is only the starting point for building common goals.

Tasks vs. Common Goals

TASKS	**COMMON GOALS**
Serves individual interests	Requires building together
Each person does their part	Must distribute: • POWER (who decides?) • AUTHORITY (who can question/act?) • RESPONSIBILITY (who does work?)

Common goals build collective capacity, but only when power moves with them. If only Carmen knew the budget, she held an advantage the others didn't. When all partners could read the financials and question expenditures, that power was shared. If only Maya controlled the data, she was the gatekeeper. When every partner could access and use it, capacity was shared.

Power is who decides. Authority is who can question and act. Responsibility is who does the work. At Sarah's table, Tres Valles held all three roles. The partners were only responsible, that's why one email could end everything.

When Maya's coalition rebuilt, they redistributed power, authority and responsibility intentionally. Carmen held fiscal authority, but every partner could question the budget. Terrence held youth programming, but Maya's data made his results visible to everyone. Decisions required consensus. No single person could pull the table out from under the rest.

This is what separates genuine partnership from coordination. Coordination assigns tasks efficiently. Partnership builds shared capacity so coalitions can do things no single organization can do alone.

Gratitude: The Glue That Generates Continued Reciprocity

Sarah kept Maya close enough to keep delivering. Early in the partnership, she communicated steadily and responded quickly, but over time that thinned. She returned calls and emails late or not at all. There were still moments of warmth, which is why the pattern was hard for Maya to see.

That is breadcrumbing: giving just enough attention and recognition to keep someone in the work without ever matching it with real commitment.

You may have experienced this yourself, perhaps from a partner with more resources. They praised your community relationships in a meeting but made the decision without you. They cited your data in the report but never mentioned where it came from. They thanked the team publicly and named everyone except the person who did most of the work. They returned your call only when they needed something.

Breadcrumbing is a power move, whether conscious or not, that erodes the conditions for trust faster than outright conflict because it is harder to name. It withholds real acknowledgment tied to real contribution and keeps the person just invested enough to stay. It drains the fuel for cooperation without revealing itself as the cause.

True gratitude isn't just about having warm feelings. It's about making specific acknowledgments that create the conditions for continued cooperation. Consider the difference between these three statements:

"Thanks to our partners for their hard work."

"Carmen taught us to read financial statements in three sessions. Now we can catch discrepancies and ask informed budget questions."

"Carmen's commitment to teaching rather than just doing the work herself showed us what partnership looks like.

Her transparency and willingness to share, and not hoard expertise, changed how we think about collaboration."

The first statement is vague: it tells you nothing. The second names concrete deliverables and outcomes. The third names Carmen's values and approach to partnership. Effective gratitude requires both the second and third approach. It values both the contributions and the person, and why they specifically matter.

Research shows gratitude and indebtedness are two sides of the same coin. When someone meets your self-interest, you feel indebted. Equity theorists have studied this for decades: people have a deep drive to balance what they give and receive, and when the exchange feels unequal, it creates tension that demands resolution.[1] You either reciprocate or you withdraw. When you express gratitude, you make that reciprocation visible. You name what was given and signal that the exchange matters. Research shows this plays an early role in relationship development because it tells the other person their effort was seen and worth repeating. Over time, that cycle becomes a building block of trust.

Gratitude also pushes back against unequal power. When a partnership only recognizes what people produce, it

---

[1] Equity theorists describe the human drive to balance what we give and receive as fundamental to sustained cooperation. For foundational work on reciprocity and social relations, see Kolm, S.-C. (2008). *Reciprocity: An Economics of Social Relations*. Cambridge University Press.; on gratitude as a driver of trust and reciprocity, see Raggio, R.D., Walz, A.M., Bose Godbole, M., and Garretson Folse, J.A. (2014). Gratitude in Relationship Marketing: Theoretical Development and Directions for Future Research. European Journal of Marketing, 48(1/2), 2-24.

reduces them to their usefulness. When it names who they are, not just what they delivered, it tells people they matter beyond the transaction. That is what separates reciprocity from exchange and how the cycle deepens into trust.

In partnerships, specific acts of gratitude serve multiple functions. They validate commitments. They reference concrete delivery. They create a public record so when funders or media come calling, there's documentation of specific contributions. They open opportunities beyond the original partnership.

How the Cycle Deepens: Why Sequential Progress Matters

You now have the three elements. What matters next is how they move together.

Trust builds through what partners do together: collaborating on events that unfold, activities they complete and choices they make in response.[2] What you do together changes how you think about each other, and that shapes what you're willing to try next. This is why we focus on cycles, so partners can follow their trajectory over time.

---

[2] Langley (1999) provides a process framework for tracking how relationships evolve through events, activities, and choices over time. Adam and Donelson's (2020) trust model extends it through the lens of self-interest, common goals, and gratitude. See Langley, A. (1999). Strategies for theorizing from process data. *Academy of Management Review*, 24(4), 691-710.

Trust grows as partners show up, follow through and take risks together. Cycles don't deepen automatically and you can't skip levels. When promises are broken and self-interests are derailed, partnerships can move backward and collapse entirely if the foundation can't hold the weight.

Progress is sequential but not linear. Partners follow the cycle in order, but every setback or new pressure can pull them back to earlier stages. That is not failure, but rather how the cycle deepens.

The levels mark the questions partners are asking. The self-assessment at the end of this book helps you locate where your partnership currently stands.

Before the first cycle, some partnerships face a prior question: Should we even try this? Some coalitions land here after betrayal or collapse, before any cycle begins. You'll know you're here when you're deciding whether to engage at all.

Cycle 1: Foundations / Can this work? Start with small, low-stakes commitments on purpose. Maya and her partners didn't begin with ambition. They began with a 48-hour communication standard and a quarterly coffee to mark meeting it. You'll know you're in Cycle 1 when you're still testing whether partners show up and follow through. Partnerships often circle back here, not because they failed but because reliability can take practice.

Cycle 2: Infrastructure / "Can this last?" Disclosures deepen. Carmen admitted she didn't want to hold things together forever. Terrence admitted he wouldn't have stayed without Maya and Carmen checking in on him. You'll know you're in Cycle 2 when you're building common goals and shared systems, and when partners are willing to be honest about what they need.

Cycle 3 and Beyond: Transformation / "Can this change how work gets done?" Self-interests expand beyond individual organizations into shared influence: shifting policy, changing practice and creating models others replicate. Gratitude becomes shared credit for changing the field. This is beyond the arc of our story, but it's where Maya's sensor work would have reached funders and policymakers looking for proven models. You'll know you're in Cycle 3 when your partnership changes how work gets done.

Trust Deepens Across Cycles: Why You Can't Skip Past Levels You and your partners will probably know intuitively what depth you're currently reaching, even when it's uncomfortable to name.

From Partnership to System

These cycles don't just operate inside a single partnership. They operate across complex adaptive systems, which are networks of interdependent actors where small shifts in one relationship ripple across the whole.

In 2025, complexity practitioner Diane Finegold, with support from Sam Bradd and Chris Yakimov, visualized the trust framework as a feedback loop operating within them (see resources at the end of this book for more).

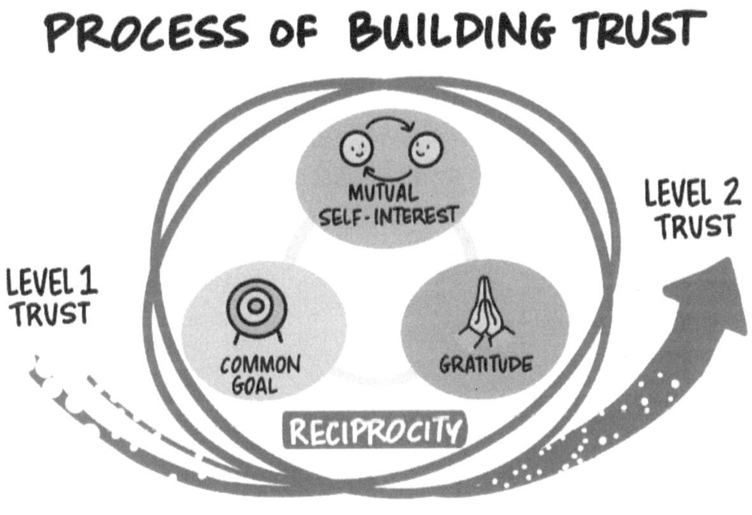

Adapted from Adam and Donelson

Frameworks Collection by finegood@sfu.ca | Illustrated by sam@drawingchange.com | © CC BY-NC-ND

Her team organizes multiple systems thinking frameworks into collections, and places ours within her *Trust and Collaboration* collection alongside others like

Organizational and Governance Strategies and *Places to Intervene*. That fit makes sense: our framework tracks how partners move from tentative, transactional relationships to deeper ones where people stay, and how those relationships influence larger systems.

Trust as a Measurement Layer

The trust-building measurement framework can lay on top of whatever engagement methodology an organization uses, following how trust moves.

Many organizations already use proven methodologies to engage communities and to bring people together to define problems, set direction and act. For example, Human Centered Design builds empathy and collective vision by centering the perspectives of those served. Appreciative Inquiry engages stakeholders by identifying strengths, possibilities and successes rather than leading with deficits. Strategic Doing (referenced in the resources at the end of this book) offers a process for forming collaborations and moving to action in open yet connected networks.

These methodologies are all aligned with the trust framework. They generate engagement, empathy and collective vision. What they don't typically measure is whether that engagement is building reciprocity or eroding it.

Two constraints shape whether trust measurement means anything at all. Power determines who controls the conditions under which trust is built or broken. Compliance sets the standard against which follow-through can actually be measured. Without both, you can generate engagement and still end up with nothing that holds.

2. Stewarding Power

In the story, Sarah set up the whiteboard, the round table and the chairs. She handed partners the MOU and walked around with the coffee pot while she talked them through page eight. She was warm, prepared and in charge of everything: the room, the document, the agenda, the budget, the access and the timeline. What looked like hospitality was architecture. One email from an attorney's office ended everything.

Partnerships like this rarely ask important questions about power until it is too late: Who designed this table? Who controls the seating? And who can move the chairs?

Power imbalances do not just stall partnerships. Unacknowledged, they create fear, and fear paralyzes people in ways that goodwill cannot fix.

Power itself is not the problem. Every partnership has it, and it is unevenly distributed; that is a fact of organizational life. The government has legal authority and funding access. Corporations have capital and political influence. Large nonprofits have staff capacity and board connections. Small community organizations have deep local trust but limited resources.

The question is not whether power exists in a partnership, but whether it is used well and held accountable. Having power doesn't make you the problem. It makes you accountable to use your resources and position to serve the partnership and to answer for how you use them. That accountability runs in every direction.

This tension shows up clearly in the most widely adopted partnership model in the field. Kania and Kramer's Collective Impact model argues effective partnerships benefit from a centralized 'backbone' organization to guide vision, align activity, establish shared measurement, build public will, advance policy and mobilize funding.[3] Those responsibilities are important, and many partnerships need some type of backbone to function.

Yet when one organization holds most or all of those functions, power quietly pools there. Backbone organizations tend to see the information first, take the calls first, and over time the gap between acting and consulting widens. As Sarah's partnership showed, this can leave everyone else dependent on whether that organization uses its position well. Critics like Tom Wolff and Vu Le have challenged this model.[4] Wolff argues it fails to address power dynamics and excludes those most

---

[3] Kania, J. and Kramer, M. (2011). Collective Impact. *Stanford Social Innovation Review.* https://ssir.org/articles/entry/collective_impact

[4] Wolff, T. (2016). Ten Places Where Collective Impact Gets It Wrong. *Global Journal of Community Psychology Practice,* 7(1). Le, V. (2015). Why Communities of Color Are Getting Frustrated with Collective Impact. Originally published on NonprofitAF.com, November 29, 2015. Reposted at https://collectiveimpactforum.org/blog/why-communities-of-color-are-getting-frustrated-with-collective-impact/

affected. Le warns that backbones become gatekeepers for funding. The field has not offered much beyond general calls for shared power. The table below proposes a different approach.

Stewarding Power Through Shared Functions

'Backbone' Convener Roles	**Roles Distributed for Achieving Common Goals**
Guide vision	Partners map self-interests, build common vision together
Manage data	Partners can access, contribute toward, and analyze data.
Coordinate activities	Partners share communication standards, decision-making authority and task allocation
Mobilize funding	Partners understand the budget, review expenditures and have opportunity to question financial decisions
Build public will	Partners share in advocacy, receive credit and control their own communications
Establish Shared Measurement Practices	Partners understand agreed upon shared standards, including compliance; progress and accountability are visible to everyone.
Advance Policy	Partners share in policy advocacy, understand how policy decisions affect the partnership and have a voice in determining which policy goals to pursue together.

Noticing When Fear Drives Decisions

Recognizing power dynamics also requires noticing when fear is driving your decisions.

Leadership researchers describe two orientations: above the line, where you lead from curiosity and accountability, and below the line, where fear and reaction can take over.

Leadership researcher Brené Brown identifies three fear-based roles people fall into when threatened: Victim, Villain, and Hero.[5] Victim thinking focuses on what happened to you, not what choices you have. Villain thinking focuses on blame, not what needs to change structurally. Hero thinking focuses on taking over, not empowering others.

You saw all three in the story. After the betrayal, Carmen couldn't stop naming villains. Terrence fell into victim thinking, replaying what they should have seen coming. Maya felt the pull to rescue everyone. These are normal human responses to fear and powerlessness. Above the line, each of those roles has a counterpart rooted in curiosity rather than fear: Creator, Challenger, and Coach. Naming which role you're in isn't about self-diagnosis.

---

[5] Brown, Brené. *Strong Ground: The Lessons of Daring Leadership, the Tenacity of Paradox, and the Wisdom of the Human Spirit.* Random House, 2025. For the above/below the line practice and the Victim, Villain, Hero framework, Brown draws on Stephen Karpman's Drama Triangle and David Emerald's Empowerment Dynamic, adapting both into her above/below the line practice. Creator, Challenger, and Coach are the above-the-line counterparts. See also brenebrown.com/resources/above-below-the-line for the visual from the book and additional citations at the end of this book.

It's about creating enough awareness to make a different choice.

Building structures doesn't make fear go away. It creates conditions where fear doesn't have to drive decisions. We have included resources on Brown's work at the end of this chapter for those who want to explore further.

Tools To Counter Fear

In the story, Sarah was afraid she couldn't pay for her child's medical care, and that fear drove her to protect herself instead of the partnership. Fear of losing a job, fear of retaliation, and fear of not being able to pay bills are all legitimate in shaping decisions. Without structures that make it safe to speak, they can silence the people who see problems first.

This is where compliance tools come in. Whistleblower protections, ethics policies and transparency expectations are federal grants management requirements, and they exist precisely because these fears are real.

Jenni and I wrote two companion workbooks, *The Money Trail: How They Lost It or Stole It* and *Lines You Shouldn't Cross: Privacy, Power and Policy*, to help teams work through these protections together. The workbooks use eight fictionalized case studies of federal grants management failures, designed for front-line staff, volunteers and board members to work through together. When everyone understands these systems, power can't concentrate as easily and fear has less room to operate.

Compliance does more than protect people who speak up. It gives partners a way to show each other the work can withstand scrutiny.

3: Proving The Cycle Holds: Compliance

Harold had seen this go wrong firsthand. He had watched a nonprofit in Cleveland shut down over a $15,000 audit finding. "The director spent the money right," he told the group, "but couldn't prove it."

That pattern is more common than most admit. Organizations do the work honestly and may have no way to prove it when it matters. They then get penalized for rules no one ever explained.

In the original partnership, none of the partners had the right documentation to protect their work. When they suspected the development authority would keep it, they had nothing to stand on. Every standard the rebuilt partnership could demonstrate was evidence of trust.

In our joint coaching and consulting work, we draw on a specific form of compliance. U.S. federal grant funds are managed under the Uniform Guidance, or 2 CFR Part 200. While designed to ensure proper stewardship of taxpayer dollars, its requirements for transparency, documented decision-making and oversight also create a best practices framework that keeps resources accountable to everyone at the table.

Most people experience federal compliance standards as burdensome: documentation, internal controls, conflict of interest policies and procurement rules. When Margaret wrote the word compliance on the whiteboard, Carmen said what most people in the room were thinking. She lived in fear of an audit finding something wrong. That fear is understandable and nearly universal. The rebuilt partnership found a different way to see it.

Compliance as the Container for Vulnerability

Compliance does more than enable proper stewardship of power. It makes trust visible, trackable and measurable as it builds or breaks down across cycles.

Margaret reframed it for the group: compliance means doing what you say you'll do, to a standard you agree on, with evidence you can point to. She showed them how it works: the partners built their common goals table with a compliance column right next to it. Many federal requirements mapped directly to work they were already building together.

When compliance is built in this way, alongside common goals rather than imposed on top of them, it becomes the container that holds vulnerability. Partners can ask hard questions, admit gaps and disclose conflicts because the standards are shared and the evidence is visible to everyone.

The Inquiry-Based Approach

Having compliance standards matters. How partners learn them together matters just as much.

When Carmen, Terrence, and Maya each took a section of compliance learning and taught the others, no single person owned all the answers anymore. Questions became safe to ask.

The coalition learned compliance through Socratic inquiry, which is working through questions together rather than deferring to one expert. They had freedom to question and learn together.

You can ask similar questions of your partners:

"Walk us through your compliance systems."

"What are my obligations as a pass-through entity?"

"How will you support us in meeting federal grants compliance standards?"

"Show us how power, authority and responsibility are being shared in this work."

If they can't answer, or won't, pay attention. That tells you something important. A partner who controls information and cannot explain how to access it is unlikely to be a good steward of it.

The Principle Applies Elsewhere

We use 2 CFR 200 as the primary example because it's the framework we know best. It's comprehensive, publicly available and tested across thousands of partnerships.

The principle works anywhere partners agree to hold each other accountable to a shared standard. Whether corporate governance, cooperative bylaws or nonprofit accountability frameworks, the protective structure is the same, requiring transparency, oversight and documentation.

The questions are the same. Can people see what's happening? Can more than one person push back on a decision? Is everything documented? Can everyone see what was promised and whether it was delivered?

You can adopt an existing compliance structure or build your own. Either way, Dusty said it best.

TRUST EVERYONE BUT BRAND YOUR CATTLE

Her hand-written note to Maya underscored the message:

Trust + Verify = Partnership

Compliance is simply doing what you said you would do, to the standard you committed to, with evidence everyone can see. It is a container that makes trust measurable. The assessment that follows helps you see what you are building and whether it will hold.

A Partnership Self-Assessment

Trust comes from a set of conditions you build, test, and tend over time. This tool helps you look honestly at those conditions in a partnership you are part of right now.

It comes in three parts:

- **Tool 1- Mutual Self-Interest:** Can needs be named, heard, and met?

- **Tool 2 - Common Goals:** Are you building shared capacity, or just dividing up tasks?

- **Tool 3 Gratitude:** Does recognition name what people actually contributed, and who they are, or does it stay generic?

Score each part as you go. At the end, you will bring the three scores together for a single picture across all the dimensions. It is not a grade. It is a mirror. It will show you where the ground is firm, where it is still soft, and where attention is needed next.

You can do this alone, but it works better with your partners. Each of you should score on your own first and then sit down to compare. The gaps across your scores are often where the real conversation begins.

Tool 1: Mutual Self-Interest

Can needs be named, heard, and met?

Instructions: Score each dimension 0–3. Read all four levels and circle the number that best describes your partnership right now. Then add your scores for a total out of 9.

Dimension 1A — Conditions for disclosure

Can all partners safely state what they need?

Score 3 Deep trust

- All partners have standing to name what they need. This is treated as essential, not optional
- Power differences are acknowledged: those with less power may need more explicit invitation, safety, and follow-through before they can disclose

- Partners recognize that anyone can silence themselves — some out of fear, some out of duty, some out of habit — and all patterns are worth noticing
- The partnership actively creates conditions for mutual disclosure from all positions

Score 2 Building

- Most partners can state needs, although some hesitate
- Power differences are recognized, even if not fully addressed
- Growing awareness that silence can come from many directions and for different reasons
- Partners are beginning to check on each other: "What do you need from this?"

Score 1 Surface level

- Only some partners feel safe naming needs
- Power differences are present but unacknowledged
- Partners self-censor for different reasons depending on their position
- Silence is assumed to mean satisfaction, or is treated as a gift rather than a gap

Score 0 Broken / red flags

- Needs only flow in one direction — or don't flow at all

- Power imbalances dictate who speaks: those with less power can't; those with more won't
- Stating needs is treated as weakness, disloyalty, or ingratitude — depending on who's speaking
- The trust cycle cannot complete because needs remain unspoken on one or more sides

Score for Dimension 1A **Your score: _____ / 3**

Dimension 1B — Disclosure of needs

Can each partner name what they actually need? Does this include internal drives and the shadow actors whose interests shape decisions from offstage?

Score 3 Deep trust

- Each partner can name multiple specific needs: both practical (funding, resources, network access, board credibility) AND internal drives (belonging, purpose, doing work that aligns with values, being seen as a whole person)
- Needs are disclosed openly without fear of judgment or seeming selfish
- Shadow actors (board members, funders, political influencers) have been identified and their interests mapped
- Partners revisit needs regularly as they evolve through cycles

Score 2 Building

- Partners can name some needs, though may be modest or incomplete
- Disclosure is happening but may focus more on practical needs than internal drives
- Some awareness of shadow actors but interests not fully mapped
- Beginning to understand that needs change over time

Score 1 Surface level

- Needs are vague ("collaboration," "capacity building") without specifics
- Partners hide deeper needs out of fear or uncertainty
- No discussion of shadow actors or their influence
- Assumption that needs stay static

Score 0 Broken / red flags

- Partners cannot or will not name what they actually need
- One partner's needs dominate while others' go unspoken
- Shadow actors control decisions but their role is hidden or denied
- Partners feel they must hide needs to remain "committed" to the partnership

Score for Dimension 1B Your score: _____ / 3

Dimension 1C — Meeting Needs

Can each partner point to something tangible they have gained? Are benefits flowing to everyone, or mostly in one direction?

Score 3 Deep trust

- Each partner can point to multiple tangible benefits received: new contracts, funding, skilled staff, media attention, policy influence, network connections that opened doors
- Benefits are documented and verifiable, not just promised
- Both practical needs and internal drives are being met (resources flowing AND people feeling valued for who they are)
- Individual success is directly attributed to the partnership, creating motivation to sustain it

Score 2 Building

- Partners can name some concrete benefits, though may be modest
- Evidence exists: one new connection, some operational support, recognition in certain contexts
- Benefits align with stated interests from initial disclosure
- Partners express satisfaction even if outcomes are still developing

Score 1 Surface level

- Partners struggle to name concrete benefits beyond "good relationships" or "learning"
- Promises made but little delivered yet (verify timeline is realistic)
- Benefits flow primarily to one or two partners, not distributed
- Vague language about "future opportunities" without specifics

Score 0 Broken / red flags

- Partners getting nothing tangible from the partnership
- One partner extracting value while others contribute without return
- Requests for resources, connections, or recognition consistently denied or delayed
- Partners stay engaged out of obligation, fear, or lack of alternatives

Score for Dimension 1C Your score: _____ / 3

Total Score: Mutual Self-Interest

Add your three dimension scores:
1A ___ + 1B ___+ 1C ___= ___/ 9

0–2 Extraction risk. Needs are hidden, unmet, or unsafe to name. Address structural problems before moving forward.

3–4 Early and fragile. Foundation is forming but disclosure is incomplete.

5–6 Building trust. Needs are being named and benefits are being felt. Watch for where disclosure still feels risky.

7–9 Deep trust. Self-interest is working, is visible, reciprocal, and distributed. Solid foundation for the rest of the framework.

Tool 2: Common Goals

Are you building shared capacity, or just dividing up tasks?

Instructions: Score each dimension 0–3. Read all four levels and circle the number that best describes your partnership right now. Then add your scores for a total out of 9.

Dimension 2A — Common goals vs. divided tasks

Are partners building collective capacity, or coordinating separate lines of work?

Score 3 Deep trust

- Multiple common goals where partners build collective capacity together (examples: all learning compliance collectively, all gaining budget literacy, all accessing shared data systems)

- Goals require all partners at the table; losing a person or organization would be felt, not just a task reassigned
- You are building something none of you has alone
- Tasks also exist, but they support common goals rather than replacing them

Score 2 Building

- Some common goals emerging alongside divided tasks
- Partners starting to learn together, though capacity is still uneven
- Beginning to build what no one had alone
- Mix of coordination (tasks) and partnership (shared capacity)

Score 1 Surface level

- Mostly divided tasks: one partner manages data, another handles fiscal, another runs programs
- Work is coordinated efficiently, but partners could do it in parallel without each other
- If someone left, their task would be reassigned vs realigned
- "Collaboration" is task coordination, not capacity building

Score 0 Broken / red flags

- Only divided tasks, no common goals
- No attempt to build shared capacity
- Partners kept in separate lanes deliberately
- Efficiency is valued over collective capability

Score for Dimension 2A Your score: _____ / 3

Dimension 2B — Information access and transparency

Can all partners independently access, read, and verify financial data and shared standards?

Score 3 Deep trust

- All partners can access applicable financial information, read budgets, and question expenditures
- All partners can access, analyze, and present data independently, not dependent on one person
- All partners understand compliance and shared standards expectations and can verify they are current
- Multiple partners have administrative access to key systems
- Documentation shows information flows to everyone

Score 2 Building

- Most partners can access key information, though some gaps remain
- Compliance systems exist and are documented; partners learning together
- Moving toward shared access even if not fully proficient
- Some information is still controlled, but the trend is toward openness

Score 1 Surface level

- Only one or two partners truly understand budgets, data, or compliance
- Others can ask questions, but cannot independently access or verify
- Information shared sporadically or only when requested
- One partner serves as gatekeeper, even if well-intentioned

Score 0 Broken / red flags

- One organization controls the budget, compliance, and data with no transparency
- Partners cannot access information even when explicitly requested
- Requests for access are denied, delayed, or met with excuses
- Information is power and power is guarded

Score for Dimension 2B Your score: ____ / 3

Dimension 2C — Decision authority distribution

Do all partners have real authority to act, or are they only asked for input after decisions have already been made?

Score 3 Deep trust

- Decision-making is genuinely distributed with documented processes
- All partners have authority to act, not just provide input
- Consensus processes exist with clear conflict resolution
- Budget modifications require agreement
- No single partner can make unilateral decisions on shared resources

Score 2 Building

- Decision processes are mostly collaborative, with occasional reversion to single-party control
- Partners have some authority, though not fully equal
- Working toward consensus even when uncomfortable
- Documented processes are emerging

Score 1 Surface level

- Partners are asked for "input" or "feedback" but don't have real decision authority

- One partner makes decisions, then presents them as collaborative
- Vague commitments to shared decision-making without clear processes
- Decisions could theoretically be reversed without consulting partners

Score 0 Broken / red flags

- One organization makes all real decisions
- Other partners are informed after decisions are made
- Token consultation that does not influence outcomes
- Authority is concentrated and defended

Score for Dimension 2C Your score: ____ / 3

Total Score: Common Goals

Add your three dimension scores: 1A ___ + 1B ___+ 1C ___= ___/ 9

0–2 Power concentrated. Tasks are divided, but no shared capacity is being built. The partnership is structured for extraction, not collaboration.

3–4 Early stage. Some common goals are emerging and transparency is improving, but decision authority is still uneven.

5–6 Building. Shared capacity is developing and information is more openly accessible. Keep closing gaps in decision authority.

7–9 Deep trust. Goals are genuinely shared, information flows freely, and decision authority is distributed. This is what collective capacity looks like.

Tool 3: Gratitude

Is recognition specific and reciprocal, or is it just enough to keep partners delivering?

Instructions: Score each dimension 0–3. Read all four levels and circle the number that best describes your partnership right now. Then add your scores for a total out of 9.

Dimension 3A — Specificity and substance

Does recognition name what people actually contributed, and who they are, or does it stay generic?

Score 3 Deep trust

- Gratitude names specific contributions: "Carmen taught us to read budgets in three sessions; now we can catch discrepancies and ask informed questions."
- Recognition acknowledges both what people delivered (outcomes) AND who they are (values, approach): "Carmen's willingness to teach rather than hoard expertise showed us what partnership looks like."

- Acknowledgment creates a public record: meeting minutes, board reports, letters of recommendation
- All partners can point to times their specific contributions were named

Score 2 Building

- Recognition happens regularly, though it may be modest
- Partners are acknowledged in some contexts: meetings, reports
- Recognition exists but isn't always specific enough to capture what each partner truly contributes.
- Partners feel their work is seen, even if recognition is still developing

Score 1 Surface level

- Recognition is vague: "thanks to our partners" without naming contributions
- Credit given privately but not publicly, where it would benefit the organization
- Generic appreciation without specifics
- Partners feel contributions are somewhat taken for granted

Score 0 Broken / red flags

- No public recognition of partner contributions
- Vague thanks with no specifics, or no thanks at all
- Lead organization takes credit for work others did
- When asked about recognition, deflection rather than acknowledgment

Score for Dimension 3A Your score: ____ / 3

Dimension 3B — Reciprocity: Does recognition open doors?

Does being recognized in this partnership translate into real opportunities, or does credit mostly flow to the lead organization?

Score 3 Deep trust

- Recognition opens tangible doors: new funders, media opportunities, policy influence, board connections
- All partners receive credit proportional to contribution, not just the lead organization
- Partners actively create opportunities for each other
- Evidence: written recommendations submitted, conference presentations naming all partners, and strategic introductions documented
- Partners celebrate each other's successes

Score 2 Building

- Some doors open as a result of recognition, building gradually
- Partners acknowledged publicly in some contexts if not always with high visibility
- Beginning to create opportunities for each other
- Evidence shows credit is shared, even if unevenly

Score 1 Surface level

- Promises of "we'll make sure you're recognized" without follow-through
- One organization receives most public credit while others remain in the background
- Recognition does not translate to new opportunities for partners
- When high-visibility chances arise, funder meetings, media, and conferences, only some partners are included

Score 0 Broken / red flags

- Partners explicitly excluded from high-visibility opportunities
- Contributions used to build one organization's reputation while others remain invisible
- Pattern of promising credit that never materializes ("next time")
- Lead organization opens doors for itself using others' work

Score for Dimension 3B Your score: _____ / 3

Dimension 3C — Mattering vs. breadcrumbing

Do partners feel valued as whole people, or only when they are producing something useful?

Score 3 Deep trust

- Partners feel valued as whole people, not just for their output
- Significance is independent of usefulness
- Recognition acknowledges who people are beyond what they deliver
- When challenges arise, partners are supported rather than dropped
- Consistent commitment through ups and downs

Score 2 Building

- Partners generally feel valued beyond transactional contribution
- Beginning to acknowledge the whole person, not just deliverables
- Support is present though may waver under pressure
- Building toward valuing people independent of productivity

Score 1 Surface level

- Appreciation seems tied to current usefulness
- When partners stop delivering, attention decreases
- Support comes when things are going well, but is uncertain when challenged
- Unclear whether the partnership would survive if a partner couldn't respond every time they were asked.

Score 0 Broken / red flags

- Clear breadcrumbing pattern: just enough support and attention to keep partners delivering, but never actual commitment
- Partners feel they matter only while useful
- When bigger opportunities appear, interests shift, and partners become suddenly invisible
- Support disappears when someone struggles or when a better opportunity emerges
- The message becomes: "You mattered only while useful."

Score for Dimension 3A Your score: _____ / 3

Total Score: Gratitude

Add your three dimension scores:

1A ___ + 1B ___+ 1C ___= ___/ 9

0–2 Extraction pattern. Recognition is absent, vague, or used to keep partners delivering without real commitment. Exit or major restructuring needed.

3–4 Early stage. Some recognition is happening, but it is not yet specific, public, or opening real doors for all partners.

5–6 Building. Recognition is becoming more specific and reciprocal. Continue making gratitude concrete and public.

7–9 Deep trust. Recognition is specific, opens real doors, and partners feel valued as whole people beyond their output.

Your Total Partnership Trust Score

What the numbers reveal about where your partnership is and what to do next.

Total Partnership Trust Score	
Tool 1: Mutual Self-Interest:	____ / 9
Tool 2: Common Goals:	____ / 9
Tool 3: Gratitude:	____ / 9
Total:	**____ / 27**

What your score means: Which cycle are you in?

22–27 points = Cycle 3 -Transformation

You have deep trust with distributed power and sustained reciprocity. You are ready for, or are already pursuing, collective transformation. Your partnership can fundamentally change how work gets done locally or beyond.

Focus Areas:

- Pursue collective impact that none of you could achieve alone
- Build governance structures that protect against capture
- Create systems designed to outlast the partnership
- Co-present, co-publish, collectively advocate
- Share credit for transformation
- Use collective power to elevate the field

Things to Consider:

- Risks only make sense if Cycles 1 and 2 are solid.
- Can you absorb conflict at this level of complexity?
- Are you staking your reputation on collective work?

15–21 points = Cycle 2 - Infrastructure

You have proven basic reliability and are building deeper infrastructure. Power is starting to distribute. You are ready to tackle resource sharing, honest disclosure of needs, and building systems that can survive personnel changes.

Focus Areas:

- Get honest about deeper needs: sustainability, capacity gaps, board pressure
- Open budgets for all partners to review
- Teach compliance and shared standards across organizations
- Distribute decision authority so multiple people can act
- Make gratitude specific and public
- Build one piece of infrastructure at a time

Things to Consider:

- This cycle requires vulnerability: Can you admit struggles?
- Are you building systems or still just coordinating tasks?
- Is gratitude opening real doors or staying performative?
- It is normal to stall here for months, do not rush

8–14 points = Cycle 1 - Foundations

You are testing whether basic partnership functions work. Focus on small commitments, reliable systems, and proving you can show up consistently.

Focus Areas:

- Establish reliable meeting patterns and communication
- Follow through on small commitments
- Name modest self-interests: learning, initial connections
- Build basic systems: documentation, accessible records
- Offer simple gratitude: emails, verbal thanks
- Watch for patterns from past partnerships

Things to Consider:

- It is normal to cycle back here multiple times, this is not failure
- Are partners showing up consistently?
- Can you name conflicts or are they going underground?

0–7 points = Should we even try? / Can this be repaired?

Trust is broken or the partnership shows serious red flags. Do not deepen commitment without major structural changes or an honest assessment of whether this partnership should exist.

Focus Areas:

- If pre-partnership: Do you have enough compatible interests to justify the risk? Can power actually be distributed here, or is concentration built into the model?
- If post-breakdown: What specifically broke? Can power be redistributed, or is the structure fundamentally flawed? Some violations may be too severe to repair.

Red Flags:

- Benefits flow one direction with no reciprocity
- Power is concentrated and defended, not distributed
- Contributions consistently go unrecognized
- Breadcrumbing pattern: enough attention to keep partners delivering but no actual commitment
- Extraction model: one organization building reputation and resources on others' work

Resources

The works listed here are ones we draw upon throughout this book and in our broader trust-building work with organizations.

They represent recent scholarship, peer-reviewed research and key thinking on trust frameworks, self-interest and the conditions that make genuine partnership possible. We recommend them to readers who want to go deeper into the theory behind the practice. Each entry includes a brief note on its relevance to the work.

Adam, M. B. & Donelson, A. J. (2020). *Trust is the Engine of Change: A Conceptual Model for Trust Building in Health Systems.* Systems Research and Behavioral Science

Original peer-reviewed framework introducing reciprocity as a measurable trust dimension, proposing a process model from tentative engagement to sustained mutual commitment. This provides the theoretical grounding for Adam and Donelson's additional peer-reviewed works at *trustforchange.org*, which includes a free downloadable manual demonstrating how communities build solutions when power, authority, and responsibility are genuinely shared.

Brown, B. (2025). *Strong Ground*. Penguin Random House

Brown's research demonstrates that you cannot skip past fear to get to trust. You have to name it first, then choose how to respond. Her work synthesizes a lineage of thinking on reactive versus grounded behavior: Karpman's Drama Triangle (1968), Emerald's Empowerment Dynamic (2005), Taylor's cultural accountability model (2005), and Dethmer, Chapman, and Warner Klemp's Above/Below the Line framework (2015). Essential to understanding the power and vulnerability dynamics in this book.

Cloud, H. (2023). *Trust: Knowing When to Give It, When to Withhold It, How to Earn It, and How to Fix It When It Gets Broken.* Worthy Books

Framework for evaluating trustworthiness using five essentials: understanding, motive, ability, character and track record. Cloud emphasizes all five must be present and that they apply to both individuals and the organizational systems within which they operate.

Donelson A. and Moreno, J. Money Trail Workbooks *(2025). The Money Trail: How they Lost It Or Stole It and Lines You Shouldn't Cross: Privacy, Power and Policy*

Practical guides in establishing federal grants management compliance best practices for front-line staff, volunteers and board members. Democratizes compliance knowledge rather than concentrating it in experts. *www.entrustsource.com*

Finegood, D., Bradd, S., & Yakimov, C. (2025). ***Complex Systems Frameworks for Trust and Collaboration***

Complex systems behave in ways that defy simple cause and effect: small changes ripple outward, patterns emerge from interactions and trust can collapse or accelerate. Finegold, Bradd, and Yakimov's practical visualizations offer an accessible entry point into this field. Captures Adam and Donelson's trust building work to help partnerships conceptualize more resilient collaboration *www.complexsystemsframeworks.ca/collections/trust-and-collaboration*

Lax, D. A. & Sebenius, J. K. (2002). ***3-D Negotiation: Powerful Tools to Change the Game in Your Most Important Deals.*** **Harvard Business School Press**

Written from the perspective of business negotiation, this is essential reading on mapping hidden stakeholders and shadow players who can influence decisions from outside the formal negotiation space. Emphasizes the critical importance of clarifying your own interests before disclosing them, and mapping all stakeholders' interests, not just those officially at the table.

Morrison, E., Hutcheson, S., Nilsen, E., Fadden, J., & Franklin, N. (2019). ***Strategic Doing: Ten Skills for Agile Leadership.*** **Wiley. (strategicdoing.net)**

Collaborative strategy framework designed for open, loosely connected networks facing complex challenges. Uses rapid experimentation, short-term commitments, and disciplined conversations to help partners identify what they can do together with assets they already have. Aligned to the trust building approaches described in this book. www.*strategicdoing.net*

Nielsen, K. B. *Liberating Organizations: Building the Case for Freedom (2025).* Entrustsource.

Demonstrates how freedom is needed to build trust within organizations. Showcases the value for all stakeholders when resilient and sustainable workplaces harness freedom, engagement and responsibility.

Ostrom, E. & Walker, J. (Eds.). (2003). *Trust and Reciprocity: Interdisciplinary Lessons from Experimental Research.* Russell Sage Foundation.

A foundational volume featuring contributions from Nobel Laureates Elinor Ostrom and Vernon Smith, drawing on behavioral psychology and game theory to examine how trust and reciprocity develop. Challenges purely self-interested models of human behavior, providing evidence that reciprocal relationships are central to how trust originates and how cooperative behavior is sustained.

Svendsen, G. T. (2025). *Trust.* Johns Hopkins University Press/Aarhus University Press.

Svendsen argues that societies and organizations with high trust spend less on control and surveillance and more on innovation and growth. His core finding, that trust expands when knowledge is shared and control is minimized, is the backbone of the compliance-as-protection argument we make throughout this book:

transparent systems free people rather than restrict them.

Wallace, J. (2023). *Never Enough: When Achievement Culture Becomes Toxic and What We Can Do About It.* Portfolio/Penguin Random House.

Journalist Jennifer Wallace builds on sociologist Morris Rosenberg's foundational research (1985) establishing mattering as a fundamental human need distinct from belonging. It requires four conditions be met: feeling significant, being appreciated for who you are, knowing others are invested in you, and being needed.

Wallace extends this into modern institutional contexts, showing what happens to people and organizations when those conditions are absent. This is directly relevant to the partnership dynamics in Part 4, where breadcrumbing and exclusion are not just strategic failures but structural ones that erode the human foundation trust requires.

GRATITUDE

Our friendship came first. This book grew from it, which feels exactly right for a book about trust.

Angie

The trust-building framework at the heart of this book grew out of a decade of collaboration with Dr. Mary Adam, a research partner, thought partner and model of what genuine co-governance looks like in practice, alongside her community health team at Kijabe Community Hospital. They gave their time and their trust to this tireless work, and I am indebted to all of them.

I owe deep gratitude to the nonprofit leaders and staff I have worked alongside for two decades. They hold the line on hard work, accountability and relationships, often with very little recognition and even less resourcing. They are the reason this work matters.

My friend and colleague Dr. Robin Breault brought rigor, incredible creativity, and a generous spirit to our applied work together. She kept me centered on the people actually doing it.

To my parents, Judy and David Buckert: you passed on a love of writing, publishing and a deep belief in those doing the little-seen work that builds trusted relationships over time.

And to my husband, Roy: you have been patient with this passion project and the years of almost done, and never quite. Thank you for believing this was worth it.

Jenni

As a young child, my mother owned a small business. I spent countless hours there helping and grew up watching her navigate some very challenging situations in systems that should have protected her and didn't. Those experiences helped shape what I pay attention to and why. I am grateful for her, and for what those years gave me, even the hard parts. Thank you, Mom, for always having a place for me there.

My husband has been my steadiest supporter through three books and the time they took. He never wavered. That kind of patience is one of the things I love most about him. Thank you for believing in me.

My daughter Judy brought the visuals in this book to life. She took our ideas and made them real. Seeing her drawings on these pages is one of my favorite things about this book.

My sisters have cheered me on from the beginning. And Jaimie Perkunas and Tracey Gutheim have been the kind of friends who consistently see my potential, challenge me to grow, and remind me to be patient and compassionate with myself along the way.

I'm deeply grateful for fifteen years of friendship with Angie before writing our books. Our partnership has asked us both to practice what we teach. We said yes to this together, and the trust framework at the heart of this work isn't abstract to either of us. We strive to live it.

WORKING WITH US

Bring Us to Your Table & Into Your Work

Donelson Consulting LLC *Angela leads and supports organizations to structure, finance, implement and evaluate complex partnerships, building stakeholder capacity to deliver on their commitments and turn collaboration into lasting trust.* ***donelsonconsulting.com***

2 CFR Clarity | *Jenni believes compliance done well is empowering, and she coaches and speaks to help organizations build the kind of culture where people understand the rules, ask good questions, and protect what they've built.* ***2cfrclarity.com***

Learn With Us

From self-guided modules to facilitated cohort programs, we offer peer mentorship training on compliance designed for the real pressures nonprofit and government teams face. Individual or combined programs available. ***money.trail@entrustsource.com***

Take It Further

Companion workbooks to put these tools to work in your organization. ***www.entrustsource.com***

www.ingramcontent.com/pod-product-compliance
Lightning Source LLC
LaVergne TN
LVHW091520200926
848483LV00002B/260
9781942308683